DEPARTMENT OF THE ENVIRONMENT

# The future management of water in England and Wales

## A report by the Central Advisory Water Committee

*LONDON*
HER MAJESTY'S STATIONERY OFFICE
1971

The Central Advisory Water Committee is appointed under section 2 of the Water Act 1945. Its functions are

   i.  advising the Secretary of State for the Environment or any other Minister concerned on matters connected with the conservation and use of water resources

   ii.  advising any Minister concerned with the administration of enactments which relate to or in any way affect the conservation or use of water resources or the provision of water supplies, upon any question that may be referred by him to the committee in connection with the operation, or proposed amendments of, the said enactments

   iii.  considering the operation of any such enactments, and making to the Minister concerned such representations with respect to matters of general concern arising in connection with the operation of those enactments, and such recommendations for their extension or modification as the Committee think fit.

SBN 11 750396 7

iv

Mr R. E. Woodward, M.B.E., Ll.M.
(Clerk and Chief Executive Officer, Mersey and Weaver River Authority)

*Assessors*
Mr I. R. H. Allan, M.A., F.I.Biol.
(Chief Officer, Salmon and Freshwater Fisheries, Ministry of
Agriculture, Fisheries and Food)

Mr J. E. Beddoe
(Under Secretary, Department of the Environment)

Mr B. H. Evans
(Assistant Secretary, Welsh Office)

Mr W. J. Glenn, C.B., B.A., B.A.I., F.I.C.E.
(Chief Engineer, Department of the Environment)

Mr E. A. G. Jonhnson, C.B.E., B.Sc.(Eng.), F.I.C.E., F.I.W.E.
Chief Engineer, Ministry of Agriculture, Fisheries and Food)

Sir Norman Rowntree, B.Sc., F.I.C.E., F.I.W.E.
(Director, Water Resources Board)

Mr A. Savage
(Assistant Secretary, Ministry of Agriculture, Fisheries and Food)

*Secretary*
Dr D. R. Lewis

*Assistant Secretaries:*
Mr D. W. Varley

Miss M. Baldwin
(Department of the Environment)

1  Mr Drew and Mr Lillicrap were appointed as additional members in October 1969.
2  Mr Henchley was appointed in June 1970
3  Lord Hirshfield resigned because of other commitments in November 1970.
4  Mr Lancaster died in April 1970.

# CONTENTS

*Paragraph*

**Preface** ... 1–10

**Chapter 1** **The present organisation**

THE DIVERSITY OF INTERESTS ... ... ... 11–15

WATER UNDERTAKERS ... ... ... ... 16–31

Regrouping ... ... ... ... ... 19–21

Finance ... ... ... ... ... ... 22–25

Local authority undertakings ... ... ... 26

Joint boards ... ... ... ... ... 27

Statutory companies ... ... ... ... 28

Control exercised by central government ... 29

Co-operation between water undertakers ... 30–31

SEWERAGE AND SEWAGE DISPOSAL AUTHORITIES ... 32–49

Finance ... ... ... ... ... ... 41–47

Management ... ... ... ... ... 48

Control exercised by central government ... 49

RIVER AUTHORITIES ... ... ... ... ... 50–58

Water conservation ... ... ... ... 54–63

Finance ... ... ... ... ... 59–60

Control exercised by central government ... 61–63

Land drainage and sea defence ... ... ... 64–72

Finance ... ... ... ... ... 69–72

Control of pollution ... ... ... ... 73–80

Finance ... ... ... ... ... 78

Control exercised by central government ... 79–80

Fisheries ... ... ... ... ... ... 81–83

Navigation and recreation ... ... ... 84–89

THE WATER RESOURCES BOARD ... ... ... 90–95

CENTRAL GOVERNMENT ... ... ... ... 96–101

**Chapter 2**    **The planning of resources**

THE NEED FOR NATIONAL PLANNING ... ... 102–110

THE IMPORTANCE OF WATER QUALITY ... ... 111–119


**Chapter 3**    **Weaknesses in the present system**

THE OBSTACLES TO SUCCESS ... ... ... 120–121

LEGISLATIVE DEFECTS ... ... ... ... 122–124

THE ADEQUACY OF THE OPERATING UNITS ... ... 125–130

River authorities ... ... ... ... ... 126

Water undertakings ... ... ... ... 127–129

Sewage disposal units ... ... ... ... 130

STRUCTURAL DEFECTS IN ORGANISATION ... ... 131–147

Inflexibility in the use of existing resources ... 132–133

Divided responsibility for new sources ... 134–139

The promotion of joint or national schemes ... 140–144

Conflicts of interest in regard to water
reclamation ... ... ... ... ... 145

Wider conflicts ... ... ... ... ... 146–147

CONCLUSION ... ... ... ... ... ... 148


**Chapter 4**    **The need for effective co-ordination**

THE NATIONAL PLAN ... ... ... ... ... 149–153

THE ACTION PROGRAMME ... ... ... ... 154–161

THE REGIONAL PLAN ... ... ... ... ... 162–164

PLANNING AND CO-ORDINATION
AS A DISTINCT FUNCTION ... ... ... ... 165–167

CONCLUSION ... ... ... ... ... ... 168


**Chapter 5**    **The alternative systems of organisation**

THE TWO APPROACHES ... ... ... ... 169–172

A SYSTEM OF ORGANISATION BASED ON
MULTI-PURPOSE AUTHORITIES ... ... ... 173–196

Finance ... ... ... ... ... ... 181–188

Public accountability ... ... ... ... 189–196

SYSTEMS OF ORGANISATION BASED ON
SINGLE-PURPOSE AUTHORITIES ... ... ... 197–244

System A ... ... ... ... ... ... 198–207

Financial considerations ... ... ... 208–212

Alternative systems of organisation based on
single-purpose authorities ... ... ... 213–215

System B ... ... ... ... ... ... 216–218

System C ... ... ... ... ... ... 219–223

Resolution of conflicts in systems based on
single-purpose authorities ... ... ... 224–236

Conclusions ... ... ... ... ... 237–244

System A ... ... ... ... ... 238–239

System B ... ... ... ... ... 240–241

System C ... ... ... ... ... 242–243

TABLE: Distribution of functions in systems
based on single-purpose authorities

Chapter 6 The role of the national water authority ... 245-258

Chapter 7 The position of Wales ... ... ... ... 259–267

Chapter 8 The area for decision

INTRODUCTION ... ... ... ... ... 268-272

THE POSITION OF LAND DRAINAGE AND FISHERIES 273–274

THE MAIN ARGUMENTS ... ... ... ... 275–294

Chapter 9 Summary of conclusions and recommendations 295–314

Acknowledgements ... ... ... ... 315

Page

Appendices
1. List of bodies and individuals who gave evidence. 87

2. Water quality: note by the Directorate of Engineering of the Department of the Environment. 91

3. Note on difficulties over the building of new
reservoirs. 99

4. Exchequer grants and the financing of sewerage
and sewage disposal: note by the Department
of the Environment. 100

Page

5. Maps showing possible boundaries for Regional
   Water Authorities

   (a) with 7 Regional Water Authorities          104

   (b) with 13 Regional Water Authorities         105

6. Diagrams illustrating the alternative systems of
   organisation.                                  106

# PREFACE

To the Rt. Hon. Peter Walker, M.B.E., M.P.,
Secretary of State for the Environment.

1. We were appointed by the then Minister of Housing and Local Government in September 1969, after a period in which the Committee had been in abeyance, and given the following terms of reference:

> To consider in the light of the Report of the Royal Commission on Local Government in England and of technological and other developments how the functions relating to water conservation, management of water resources, water supply, sewerage, sewage disposal and the prevention of pollution now exercised by river authorities, public water undertakings, and sewerage and sewage disposal authorities can best be organised; and to make recommendations.

2. In October 1969 we circulated a memorandum containing questions about present and future organisation to a large number of national bodies and invited them to submit evidence on these questions. We also published a general invitation to submit evidence. In all, we received written evidence from 94 bodies and 6 individuals, and these are listed in appendix 1. As indicated their 17 bodies subsequently gave oral evidence.

3. In addition to the sessions at which we took oral evidence we have met 18 times as a full Committee and a Sub-Committee met 9 times. We also visited the offices of the Water Resources Board at Reading, and discussed with the Chairman, members of the Board and senior staff the work of the Board and their views about organisation.

4. The Sub-Committee co-opted Mr S. W. Hill as a member because of his extensive knowledge of the finances of public authorities and he subsequently attended a number of meetings of the full Committee. We greatly valued his assistance.

5. In order to limit our task to one of manageable proportions, we have found it necessary to adhere as strictly as possible to the terms of reference quoted above. We were not asked to say how the future demand for water ought to be met, or what steps ought to be taken to improve the state of our rivers. Rather we were asked to recommend a system of organisation under which these objectives can be achieved. Nor were we asked to examine the organisation of specialised aspects of water services such as training and research. Important as these are in their own right, a consideration of them was not essential for our own particular purposes, though we had to keep them in mind as background to the organisational problem.

6. Our terms of reference required us to examine the organisation of the various water services in the light of the Report of the Royal Commission on Local Government in England (the Redcliffe-Maud Report)[1] and of technological and other developments. The Redcliffe-Maud Report, which was published in June 1969, recommended the establishment of a new pattern of local authorities in England outside Greater London. Its recommendations in relation to water services were that they should continue to be organised as at present except for the transfer to the new and larger local authorities of the functions exercised, individually or jointly, by the present local authorities.

1 Cmnd. 4040.

7. However, in its final report,[1] published in 1962, the Sub-Committee on the Growing Demand for Water (the Proudman Committee) drew attention to two factors. One was the increasing demand for water for all purposes. Demand has continued to increase roughly in line with the Committee's predictions and is expected to double by the end of the century. The other factor was the diversity of interests concerned with water. The Proudman Committee concluded that without overall planning it would be impossible to meet the increased demand. The present situation as regards water services is in several respects both more difficult and more complex than it was in 1962, and we therefore felt that it was necessary for us to examine in detail the structure and the deficiencies of the present system of organisation before we could proceed further. It gradually emerged that, although considerable advances have been made in overall planning, there is no effective mechanism for ensuring that plans are implemented. In other words there was an essential element missing from the Redcliffe-Maud recommendations, and we found that we had to examine much more far-reaching proposals.

8. We understand that the government agree with the Redcliffe-Maud Commission on the need for the reorganisation of local government, and with much of the analysis in its report of the problems arising from the present structure, but that they do not favour the new pattern of local authorities the Commission recommended. The government's own proposals for the new pattern of local authorities in England and Wales have not been published at the time of writing, and we have not therefore been in a position to relate our conclusions to them. However, the issues of principle involved in the proper organisation of water services will be easily apparent from our report. The further tasks of, for example, drawing detailed boundaries in the event of its being decided that local authorities should or should not retain responsibilities for water supply and sewage disposal would involve detailed investigation and consultation at the local level, something which in any case we were not qualified to undertake.

9. The structure of our report is as follows. In chapter 1, we describe in some detail the various types of body mentioned in our terms of reference. In chapter 2, we discuss the case for, and the present arrangements for, overall planning. In chapter 3, we describe the conflicts of interest which at the moment hinder the implementation of plans. Chapter 4 is devoted to setting out the kind of planning and co-ordination we consider to be necessary in future. Chapter 5 describes the different systems of organisation that might be set up to achieve this planning and co-ordination. In chapter 6, we discuss the role we envisage will be played in future by a national water authority. Chapter 7 deals with the position of Wales. For reasons which we give in chapter 8 we have been unable to reach a unanimous view as to which of the systems of organisation described in chapter 5 should be adopted. We have therefore devoted chapter 8 to setting out the main factors which ought to be taken into account in choosing between them. Chapter 9 is a summary of conclusions and recommendations.

10. In presenting our report, we wish to emphasise the urgency of the

1 Central Advisory Water Committee, Sub-Committee on the Growing Demand for Water. Final Report. HMSO, 1962.

2

problems involved in ensuring that water supplies are adequate. In considering the question of how best to organise water services, we have had to have regard to the position up to the end of the century and we believe that the sets of measures we advocate would deal with the long term problems. But since new legislation will be required to implement them, these proposals leave the present situation unaffected, and it is one of increasing urgency. Until new legislation is passed, it will be impossible to set up new bodies or to increase the present powers of existing bodies. It will therefore be essential, in the interim period, to use existing powers to their maximum in order to speed up projects which are at present under consideration but not yet authorised, since otherwise serious shortages of water are likely to occur in many parts of the country during the present decade.

# 1. THE PRESENT ORGANISATION

## THE DIVERSITY OF INTERESTS

11. Our terms of reference required us to look at three types of body: statutory water undertakers, sewerage and sewage disposal authorities, and river authorities. In order to provide a basis for the later chapters of our report we devote this chapter to a description of them as they exist at present:

(i) **statutory water undertakers** of which there are 198 in England and Wales, are under statutory obligations to provide supplies of piped water for domestic and non-domestic consumers. We describe them in paras. 16-31;

(ii) **sewerage and sewage disposal authorities** of which there are over 1,300 in England and Wales, are either local authorities or in a few cases joint boards of local authorities. We describe them in paras. 32-49;

(iii) **river authorities** of which there are 29, are responsible for water conservation under the Water Resources Act 1963, and also for land drainage, fisheries, the control of pollution and in some cases navigation. We describe them in paras. 50-87.

12. In addition to these three types of body there are a number of other public bodies which, although not mentioned in our present own terms of reference, perform functions in relation to water. These include:

(i) the **government departments** concerned with water, to which we refer in paras. 96-101;

(ii) the **Water Resources Board,** the central body established under the Water Resources Act 1963, to which we refer in paras. 90-95;

(iii) the **British Waterways Board,** a public corporation which owns the great bulk of the canals in Great Britain and is also the navigation authority for some navigable rivers. In addition to its responsibilities for navigation (see para. 89) the Board sells water from its canals, and receives into them substantial discharges of effluents and surface water. Sales of water account for about one sixth of its income;

(iv) there are a number of other bodies, apart from river authorities and the British Waterways Board, which are **navigation authorities** for particular stretches of river, or own particular canals;

(v) **local authorities,** whether or not they are sewerage or sewage disposal authorities, have certain land drainage powers (see paras. 66-67). They may also wish to develop particular stretches of water for the purposes of amenity or recreation: for example, rivers are likely to be a central feature in many of the country parks established under the Countryside Act 1968;

(vi) **internal drainage boards** are responsible under the general supervision of the relevant river authority for the drainage of certain low-lying areas which derive benefit, or avoid danger, as a result of drainage operations. They deal with local problems of land drainage by improving and maintaining the main drains and, where necessary, by pumping water from low-lying land into the river authority's main river or directly into the sea. This work, and the regulatory control which the boards exercise through byelaws, complement the operations which farmers carry out on their field drains and ditches. There are 368 internal drainage districts in 24 river authority areas, and they cover in all 3¼m. acres.

13. There are a number of other bodies or categories of people whose activities are directly related to water resources and who have to be taken into account in considering their management:

(i) the **Central Electricity Generating Board** uses very large quantities of water. Water used for direct cooling of power stations is all returned to source little changed in quality. Where the source of water is insufficient for a large power station, cooling towers are installed so that water can be reused. This leads to a great reduction in the quantity abstracted but to the loss of some of it by evaporation from the cooling towers. According to the CEGB's evidence to us power stations abstract on average 13,600 million gallons per day, of which 5,200 mgd is non-saline and the remainder is drawn from estuaries and the sea. All but 54 mgd of the non-saline water is returned to source;

(ii) **industrial firms** require water, sometimes in very large quantities, both for cooling and for use in industrial processes. Much of the water is discharged after use direct to rivers, streams or canals (under the terms of consents issued by river authorities), or to the sea. This may cause pollution, the extent of the pollution depending on the nature of the process in which the water has been used and the amount of treatment carried out before discharge;

(iii) to the traditional demands of **farmers and growers** for water there has more recently been added a demand for the purposes of spray irrigation. The increasing use of fertilisers and the growth of intensive livestock units have given rise to pollution problems;

(iv) **fishermen** require water and watercourses to be managed in a way which will support fish life, provide spawning grounds, support fish farms, permit the passage of migratory fish and facilitate fishing;

(v) in addition, rivers, streams, lakes and reservoirs provide important amenities. Increasing numbers of people want to use them for **sport and recreation,** other than fishing.

14. The licensing system established under the Water Resources Act 1963 has for the first time made it possible to estimate the amounts of water abstracted from inland sources by different categories of user. The following table shows the gross amounts which it is estimated were abstracted for different

6

purposes under licences issued by river authorities in the year ending 30
September 1969:

|  | Quantity | Percentage |
|---|---|---|
| public water supply | 3,000 mgd | 21.7 |
| direct industrial abstraction | 3,150 | 22.7 |
| CEGB | 7,600* | 55.0 |
| agriculture (including spray irrigation) | 60 | 0.4 |
| miscellaneous | 30 | 0.2 |
| Total: | 13,840 | 100.0 |

* includes about 3,000 mgd abstracted under licence from brackish or
   saline sources
   Source: Water Resources Board

In addition to the water which industrial users abstract direct from surface
and underground sources, they are also estimated to take about 30 per cent
of the water abstracted for public water supply.

15. We now give a detailed description of the three types of body mentioned in our terms of reference. It should be emphasised however that
this description is not intended to be in any way exhaustive. What we have
done is select the features which seem to be most significant for our purposes.

## WATER UNDERTAKERS

16. Statutory water undertakers fall into three types: companies, local
authorities and joint boards of local authorities. The following table shows
the number of undertakers of each type and the quantities of water they
supply:

|  |  | quantity supplied |
|---|---|---|
| local authorities |  |  |
| county borough councils* | 29 | 694 mgd |
| borough councils | 17 | 58 |
| urban district councils | 9 | 6 |
| rural district councils | 9 | 5 |
|  | 64 | 763 |
| joint boards | 101 | 1,499 |
| statutory companies | 33 | 636 |
| Total: | 198 | 2,898 |

* Including Anglesey C.C.

figures for 1969 adjusted to take account of subsequent regrouping
Source: Department of the Environment

17. A statutory water undertaker has a statutory duty to provide domestic
consumers in his area of supply with a wholesome supply of water, and
a similar duty to meet the needs of industrial and other non-domestic
consumers subject to satisfactory terms being agreed and provided that the
supply to domestic consumers is not thereby endangered. In order to dis-

charge their duty to domestic consumers, undertakers usually sterilise water, normally by chlorination, and in many cases they also carry out other forms of treatment; most undertakers treat all the water they supply to the standards required for drinking purposes, but some also supply water of a lower standard for industrial purposes. The greater part of the water used in industrial processes is at present obtained by direct abstraction from surface and underground sources, but the proportion obtained from water undertakings is believed to be increasing.

18. Besides statutory undertakers there are a number of small private systems of supply. They are normally in rural areas and most of them were constructed to serve landed estates: the great majority serve fewer than a hundred people. They are being rapidly taken over by statutory undertakers because their present owners are unwilling to accept the responsibility and expense of maintaining them. There is no comprehensive information available about them.

## Regrouping

19. The number of statutory water undertakers has been drastically reduced since the second world war in accordance with a deliberate government policy. At the end of the war they numbered well over a thousand. The White Paper "A National Water Policy",[1] published in 1944, proposed that there should be a much smaller number of undertakings each large enough to employ full-time expert staff and promote major capital projects: the necessary machinery for regrouping was provided in the Water Act 1945. In September 1956, however, there were still 1,030 undertakings in England and Wales and the ministry issued a circular[2] calling for faster progress. It is from this circular that regrouping dates for practical purposes. In 1958 a further circular[3] said that the minister was reasonably satisfied with progress but wanted to see a further acceleration and where necessary would use his compulsory powers under the 1945 Act. In the event, however, the use of compulsory powers has been necessary only in a small proportion of cases.

20. The regrouped undertakings have not had to satisfy any defined criteria, for example in terms of area or population, beyond those set out in the 1944 White Paper. In practice the starting-point has generally been the "water areas" suggested by the Engineering Inspectorate of the ministry in surveys carried out in the early post-war years, but the ministry have been prepared to accept different areas, especially where there was unanimous agreement locally. A subsidiary object of regrouping has been to create undertakings which cover both urban and rural areas, so that the former would be able to subsidise the higher costs incurred in the latter. There has been no particular policy about the form of a regrouped undertaking (whether it should be owned by a company, local authority or joint board), and this has therefore depended on the types and relative size of the undertakings involved. The following table compares the number of undertakers of each type in 1956 and in 1970:

1   Cmnd. 6515
2   Ministry of Housing and Local Government Circular 52/56.
3   Ministry of Housing and Local Government Circular 41/58.

|                          | 1956 |       | 1970 |     |
|--------------------------|------|-------|------|-----|
| local authorities        |      |       |      |     |
| county borough councils  | 53   |       | 29   |     |
| borough councils         | 177  |       | 17   |     |
| urban district councils  | 295  |       | 9    |     |
| rural district councils  | 358  |       | 9    |     |
|                          |      | 883   |      | 64  |
| joint boards             | 42   |       | 101  |     |
| statutory companies      | 90   |       | 33   |     |
| miscellaneous            | 15   |       | —    |     |
|                          |      | 1,030 |      | 198 |

Source: Department of the Environment

21. There is evidence that not all the undertakings created by this regrouping are large enough to be efficient in the conditions that now exist, and there have been some further amalgamations between regrouped undertakings. In terms of population served, the present size distribution of undertakings is as follows:

| population served | local authorities | joint boards | statutory companies | Total |
|-------------------|-------------------|--------------|---------------------|-------|
| under 50,000      | 26                | 6            | 2                   | 34    |
| 50,000-100,000    | 9                 | 21           | 3                   | 33    |
| 100,000-250,000   | 12                | 49           | 15                  | 76    |
| 250,000-1m.       | 14                | 24           | 11                  | 49    |
| over 1m.          | 3                 | 1            | 2                   | 6     |
|                   |                   |              | Total:              | 198   |

figures for 1969 adjusted to take account of subsequent regrouping
Source: Department of the Environment

**Finance**

22. The amount of water supplied by statutory water undertakers has increased from 1,827 mgd in 1955 to 2,899 mgd in 1969, and it continues to increase. They have therefore incurred heavy capital investment in order to keep pace with this demand. In recent years capital expenditure has been as follows:

|         | local authorities and joint boards £m | statutory companies £m | Total £m |
|---------|----------------------------------------|------------------------|----------|
| 1963/64 | 38.5                                   | 12.3                   | 50.8     |
| 1964/65 | 42.0                                   | 16.2                   | 58.2     |
| 1965/66 | 44.0                                   | 14.1                   | 58.1     |
| 1966/67 | 48.6                                   | 8.0                    | 56.6     |
| 1967/68 | 52.7                                   | 9.3                    | 62.0     |
| 1968/69 | 49.5                                   | 12.6                   | 62.1     |
| 1969/70 | 56.6                                   | Not available          |          |

Source: Department of the Environment

Revenue expenditure in recent years is shown in the following table:

| | local authorities and joint boards | | statutory companies | |
|---|---|---|---|---|
| | loan charges £m | running costs £m | capital charges* £m | running costs £m |
| 1964/5 | 31.1 | 57.0 | 6.1 | 14.4 |
| 1965/6 | 34.8 | 59.0 | 6.8 | 15.9 |
| 1966/7 | 38.1 | 64.4 | 9.3 | 16.3 |
| 1967/8 | 40.5 | 67.7 | 10.3 | 19.3 |
| 1968/9 | 45.3 | 74.2 | 10.2 | 21.3 |

* gross interest and dividends plus appropriations to internal funds, less interest received

Sources: Local Government Financial Statistics, Department of the Environment

23. There are exchequer grants under the Rural Water Supplies and Sewerage Acts towards expenditure on the initial provision of piped water in rural areas (see appendix 4, paras. 1-3). In addition, where a development serves predominantly agricultural needs, the Ministry of Agriculture may make a supplementary grant. Exchequer grants are also made towards expenditure which benefits new or expanding industry in a development area or intermediate area, or is made necessary by a town expansion scheme. All these grants, however, together represent only a small fraction of the total expenditure incurred by water undertakers.

24. Thus the income of water undertakers comes almost entirely from the charges they make to consumers of water: these are based either on the rateable value of the property occupied by the consumer ('water rates') or on metered quantity. Water supplied for industrial purposes is normally metered, and sometimes that supplied to commercial and agricultural users and very large domestic users: but apart from one small area (Malvern UD) the ordinary domestic consumer pays a water rate. The case for universal metering was considered by a Sub-Committee of the Central Advisory Water Committee which reported in 1963,[1] it concluded that universal metering was not worthwhile given the cost of the water supplied and that there was no other basis for charging which would offer any advantage over rateable value. Research is at present being carried out at Malvern and other places into the effect of metering on the demand for water but no firm results are yet available.

25. At the moment most water rate poundages are in the range 1s. 0d. to 2s. 6d., and most meter charges are in the range 2s. 0d. to 5s. 0d. per 1,000 gallons. The standard practice is to fix the rate poundage so that domestic consumers as a whole pay the same amount per unit quantity of water as metered consumers. Most undertakers make domestic consumers pay a minimum charge, regardless of rateable value, and this is usually between 30s. and 50s. a year.

1 Central Advisory Water Committee, Sub-Committee on Water Charges. Report. HMSO, 1963.

## Local authority undertakings

26. The three types of undertaker differ somewhat in their characteristics. The Public Health Act 1936 gives county borough and county district councils power to supply water within their own areas, subject to obtaining the minister's approval. Before regrouping, these powers were widely used, the management of the undertaking normally forming part of the duties of the council's Engineer and Surveyor. The typical post-regrouping local authority undertaker, however, is a county borough which has obtained powers by means of an Act or Order to supply water outside its own boundaries. The undertaking is usually administered by separate committee of the council and has its own chief officer, who is an engineer. Because water supply counts as a trading service and is financially self-supporting, the Water Committee tends to have more autonomy than other committees. (The relevant Act or Order often places restrictions on subsidising water supply or applying profits from it, and these practices are now rare). Occasionally a Water Committee has co-opted members to represent that part of the area of supply which lies outside the authority's own boundaries, but this is unusual.

## Joint boards

27. A joint board is a separate legal entity, operating under a local Act or an Order under the Water Acts. The great bulk of its membership is appointed by the county borough and county district councils in its area in rough proportion to their population or rateable value: but there are often also members appointed by the relevant county council or councils. Joint boards have normally been formed to take over a number of small undertakings, and have then had the task of welding these into an efficient system capable of meeting all the demands that will be made on it. A joint board generally has either two or three chief officers: an engineer-manager, and either a clerk and a treasurer or a clerk/treasurer. In some of the smaller boards the administrative and financial officers are part-time.

## Statutory companies

28. Companies operate under local Acts. Most of the earliest undertakers were companies, but apart from important individual examples on the north east coast, in the west Midlands and in the Bristol area, the surviving companies are heavily concentrated in south east England. There may be a general manager qualified as an engineer, as an accountant or company secretary, or as a chemist; alternatively, there may be an engineer and a secretary with equal status. The directors of a water company are usually drawn from the area which the company serves: a general manager is often a director. All share capital has to be issued by auction or tender, so as to ensure that it fetches the best price available. The rate of dividend payable on both ordinary and preference capital, and the rate of interest payable on loan capital, is controlled by the minister. The amounts which may be put to the reserve and contingency funds, and the amount of the carry forward, are limited by reference both to annual appropriations and to overall maxima. As a corollary to these limitations and the restrictions on dividends companies are required to apply any surplus income in the reduction of charges.

11

## Control exercised by central government

29. All statutory water undertakers need the minister's approval before they can develop a new source of water, and those (the great majority) who operate under a local Act or Order, rather than under the Public Health Acts, have to apply to him for an Order under the Water Acts. Alternatively, in the case of a very large project, or if there is some special difficulty, a water undertaker may promote a private Bill. A private Bill will normally contain the necessary provision for the financing of a project, and this is also sometimes done in an Order. In other cases, a local authority or joint board has to apply to the minister for loan sanction before it can borrow money to meet capital expenditure. A company does not need loan sanction, but the minister's consent is needed to any increase in its authorised capital, and the amount it can borrow on the market bears a prescribed ratio (usually 1:1) to its authorised capital. The maximum rate and charge (and usually also the minimum rate and charge) which an undertaker operating under a local Act or Order may levy are prescribed in his Act or Order and can only be altered by an Order or by a private Bill: alterations cannot normally be made at intervals of less than five years.

## Co-operation between water undertakers

30. The number of bulk supplies given by one water undertaker to another has been greatly reduced by regrouping but is still large. Often this is merely a convenient way of meeting the needs of an area near the boundaries of an undertaker's area of supply and remote from the main distribution network. Another device in such circumstances is a 'fringe order', under which one undertaker is authorised to supply water in another undertaker's statutory area of supply. In other cases a major part of an undertaker's total supplies may be obtained as a bulk supply. Manchester CB, for example, is under an obligation to supply twelve other undertakers in Lancashire and Cheshire with a total of about 32 mgd from its Lake District aqueducts, and in one case provides as much as 9.5 mgd to an undertaker with a total demand of 26 mgd. Bulk supply agreements made under the Water Acts require the minister's approval, and this is normally also required under analogous provisions in local Acts. The minister also has the power to make an Order requiring a bulk supply to be given.

31. In a certain number of cases the development of a source has been carried out jointly by two or more water undertakers. There are nine joint authorities, joint boards or formal joint committees formed by water undertakers to manage sources of this kind. An example is the Derwent Valley Water Board, which owns a group of large reservoirs on the upper reaches of the Derbyshire Derwent: the constituent authorities are Leicester CB, Nottingham CB, Sheffield CB and the South Derbyshire Water Board, and in addition a bulk supply is given to the North Derbyshire Water Board.


## SEWERAGE AND SEWAGE DISPOSAL AUTHORITIES

32. The subject of sewage disposal has recently been examined by the Working Party on Sewage Disposal (the Jeger Committee) and we are able

to refer the reader to their report for detailed background information.[1] We are much indebted to the Working Party for this examination, as this is a subject which is of fundamental importance to our own particular task.

33. At present sewerage, and sewage and trade effluent disposal, are the responsibility of more than 1,300 county borough and county district councils. Under the Public Health Act 1936 they have a duty:

> to provide such public sewers as may be necessary for effectually draining their district for the purpose of this Act and to make such provision by means of sewage disposal works or otherwise as may be necessary for effectually dealing with the contents of their sewers.

In Greater London, broadly speaking, the Greater London Council is responsible for trunk sewers and for disposal and the London boroughs are responsible for local sewers. Except in the case of those local authorities near the coast which make discharges to the sea or to uncontrolled estuaries, the standard to which a local authority must treat the contents of its sewers is governed by the terms of the consent to discharge issued to it by the river authority (see paras. 74-5).

34. There is a very wide variation in the size of the population served by an authority, from 7.7m in the case of the GLC to less than a thousand in the smallest rural district, and there is a parallel variation in the size and type of treatment plant operated. In all there are some 5,000 treatment works in England and Wales, of which 80 per cent serve populations of 10,000 or less.

35. The general conditions under which a trade effluent may be discharged into a public sewer are laid down in the Public Health (Drainage of Trade Premises) Act 1937 and the Public Health Act 1961. The approval of the sewerage authority in the form of a consent or agreement is required, and before giving it the authority must obtain the views of any other interested body such as a joint sewerage board (see para. 38). In giving its approval the authority may impose conditions (and also charges, see para. 45). There is a right of appeal to the minister against the refusal of approval or the conditions imposed. Trade effluents constitute a substantial proportion of the dry weather flows treated by sewage disposal works, on average about a fifth but in individual cases as much as a half or more.

36. Every sewerage system is designed to receive a certain amount of surface water. A 'separate' system is intended as far as possible to take only foul sewage but because of unauthorised and accidental connections it is usual to provide a capacity of between four and six times the dry weather flow. A 'combined' system is designed to receive and transmit all the drainage from the area it serves including the surface water from impermeable surfaces. 'Intermediate' or 'partially separate' systems are designed to receive and transmit a proportion of the surface water from the drainage area. Separate and partially separate systems are usually supplemented by surface water sewers; and it is common practice in combined and partially separate systems to economise on the size of sewers, and relieve sewage disposal works of

---

1 Ministry of Housing and Local Government and Welsh Office, Working Party on Sewage Disposal. **Taken for Granted.** HMSO, 1970.

storm flows in excess of certain limits, by providing overflows discharging to surface water sewers or into ditches and streams. Modern practice favours the separate system where it is practicable but most urban areas have a mixture of all three systems developed over the years. Discharges of storm sewage into ditches and streams are subject to the consent of the relevant river authority, which may for example prescribe the minimum flow that must go forward for treatment at the disposal works or specify standards of quality.

37. In the first instance sewers are constructed by developers, or by frontagers in private streets, and such sewers are known as 'on-site' sewers. The local authority provides public sewers to connect with these on-site sewers and has powers to construct such 'off-site' sewers on private land. In addition a local authority may at any time adopt any private sewer within its area, and this power is continually being exercised.

38. The design of major sewerage systems is constrained by the location of natural watersheds, which are usually not related to local authority boundaries. This has been an important factor in the formation of joint sewerage boards to administer trunk sewers and sewage disposal: there are 24 such boards, the majority formed before the first world war. The largest, the Upper Tame Main Drainage Authority, serves over 2m people in Birmingham and the surrounding area, the smallest fewer than 10,000 people. Like a joint water board, a joint sewerage board is a separate legal entity operating under a local Act or Order and the constituent local authorities normally appoint members in rough proportion to their rateable value. The Public Health Act 1936 gives the minister the power to establish a joint board compulsorily; and this power was strengthened in the Rivers (Prevention of Pollution) Act 1951 provided there are reasons for the establishment of a joint board connected with the prevention of river pollution. Only one board has been established under these powers, the Mid-Calder and Hyndburn Joint Sewerage Board, which serves the Burnley area and came into operation on 1 April 1970.

39. Even where there is not a joint board, a local authority sometimes arranges for the flows from all or part of its area to be treated at the works of a neighbouring authority. In that case, as with a joint board, the authority in whose area the flows originate remains responsible for local sewers.

40. The local authorities concerned have not always been able to provide the main sewerage, sewage disposal and surface water drainage works required for the development of a new town, and in these cases the minister has given the new town development corporation the power to provide these facilities itself by means of an Order under the New Towns Act.[1] At the moment thirteen corporations are exercising such powers. The intention is that the works should in due course be transferred to the local authorities concerned, and two such transfers have taken place.

---

1　There is also power under the New Towns Act to enable development corporations to provide water supplies: because of regrouping, this power has been seldom used and no corporation is now acting as a water undertaker.

**Finance**

41. In recent years capital expenditure by local authorities on sewerage and sewage disposal has been as follows:

| | £m |
|---|---|
| 1963/64 | 52.1 |
| 1964/65 | 63.6 |
| 1965/66 | 63.1 |
| 1966/67 | 73.2 |
| 1967/68 | 92.9 |
| 1968/69 | 101.3 |
| 1969/70 | 109.1 |

Source: Department of the Environment

In 1968/69, their revenue expenditure was £106.7m, of which £56.5m was loan charges and £50.2m running costs.

42. Unfortunately the statistics of total expenditure do not distinguish between sewerage and sewage disposal. It was, however, estimated by the Water Pollution Research Laboratory that capital expenditure by sewage disposal authorities on disposal in 1967 was about £35m and running costs about £15m. Capital expenditure by sewerage and sewage disposal authorities on sewers would then have been about £60m. It has been estimated that total annual capital expenditure on underground drainage systems (including highway sewers, and on-site drains and sewers provided by developers) is now of the order of £200m.

43. There are considerable variations between areas in the cost of sewerage and sewage disposal. The variations mainly arise from differences in the cost of sewerage, which are determined by the adequacy of the system, the date when the sewers were constructed, the length of sewer per house and the extent to which pumping is necessary. There are also wide variations, however, in the cost of sewage disposal, depending on the amount of treatment given to sewage and to sludge, the difficulties of sludge disposal, and the size and age of the works. Figures given in the report of the Jeger Committee show that the major part of the cost of sewage disposal is accounted for by treatment up to what is known as Royal Commission standard.[1] If a river authority requires the final effluent to reach a higher standard than this, the cost of additional treatment by conventional methods is relatively small, say 15 to 25 per cent more.

44. The specific exchequer grants available for sewerage and sewage disposal parallel those available for water supply (para. 23): grants under the Rural Water Supplies and Sewerage Acts towards the initial sewering of rural areas, and grants towards the cost of sewerage and sewage disposal works in development areas, intermediate areas and town expansion schemes. The rural grants are described in appendix 4. In 1967/8, the total amount received in grants was £2.7m.

---

1 Because it was proposed by the Royal Commission on Sewage Disposal which sat from 1898 to 1915. To comply with this standard an effluent should contain not more than 30 milligrams per litre of suspended solids and have a BOD of not more than 20mg/1. The standard assumes that the effluent will be diluted with 8 times its volume of clean water having a BOD of not more than 2mg/1.

15

45. As noted above an authority may (and the G.L.C. must) levy charges on dischargers of trade effluents for the conveyance of the effluents through the sewers and their subsequent treatment. The policies of individual local authorities about charges vary: where charges are made, they are based on a formula designed to reflect the cost of treatment. There is a right of appeal to the minister against charges imposed by an authority. If additional treatment capacity has to be installed to treat trade effluents the discharger may make a capital contribution. In 1967/8 the total income of authorities in England and Wales from trade effluent charges and from other earmarked sources (other than exchequer grants) was £6.3m.

46. Sewerage and sewage disposal are primarily financed therefore from the general rate. Joint sewerage boards precept on their constituent authorities. The variations in costs mean that there are also considerable variations in the rates levied for these purposes. The statistics of the Institute of Municipal Treasurers and Accountants for 1969/70 include rates as low as 1d. in the £ (for a county borough and for a non-county borough) and as high as 6s. 10d. in the £ (for a rural district).

47. Expenditure on these services is taken into account in determining the aggregate of exchequer assistance to local authorities through the Rate Support Grant: the resources element of this grant, which compensates local authorities whose penny rate product per head of population is below the average for England and Wales by meeting an appropriate proportion of their rate-borne expenditure, constitutes in a sense a percentage grant on these and other services.[1] The amount a local authority receives from this source, however, depends on its total rate-borne expenditure and its rateable value per head, and bears no necessary relationship to its expenditure on sewerage and sewage disposal.

## Management

48. In a local authority, sewerage and sewage disposal have traditionally been among the responsibilities of the Engineer and Surveyor, who is under the control of a public works committee or a committee with some similar title. A few large authorities have established a separate committee to control their sewage disposal works and have made the manager an independent chief officer. The general trend towards a reduction in the number of committees and chief officers in local authorities is, however, tending to lead to the disappearance of such arrangements where they exist. At the other extreme the largest of the joint boards, the Upper Tame Main Drainage Authority, has four chief officers: a clerk, an engineer and a chemist, with the Birmingham City Treasurer acting as treasurer.

## Control exercised by central government

49. The issue of loan sanctions (which authorise borrowing to finance capital expenditure) has traditionally been the means of achieving both the main objectives of central government control over sewerage and sewage disposal: regulation of the overall level of public sector investment and examination of the technical adequacy of schemes. 'Small' schemes, however, are not

1 The Rate Support Grant is described in more detail in appendix 4.

now subjected to technical examination: Ministry of Housing and Local Government Circular 19/63 defined small schemes, broadly speaking, as those costing not more than £30,000 or the product of a 2d. rate, whichever was higher; and Circular 48/70 (Welsh Office Circular 58/70) raised these figures to £100,000 or the product of a 2.4d. rate. On 1 April 1971 a new system will come into effect, under which the two objectives of central control will be kept largely distinct. Each London borough, county borough and county will be given a block allocation of capital payments covering the bulk of local authority services, and within this allocation will be able to use a general loan consent contained in the relevant circular[1]. Central government will, however, continue to examine individual projects within a Key Sector containing primarily those services for which ministers have special responsibilities in determining standards or co-ordinating development on a national basis; local authorities will be able to make use of a general loan consent but ministerial approval of a specific project will be required in order to activate it. In sewerage and sewage disposal 'small' schemes as defined above will be financed from the block allocations. Other schemes will fall into the Key Sector and will require the minister's specific approval on the basis of a technical examination. The new arrangements will not apply to joint sewerage boards; in their case both aspects of control will continue to be exercised through the present loan sanction procedure.[2]


## RIVER AUTHORITIES

50.  River authorities were set up under the Water Resources Act 1963 and came into operation on 1 April 1965. Of the 29 river authorities 27 were nominally new bodies which took over the responsibilities for land drainage, fisheries, the control of pollution and in a few cases navigation previously exercised by 32 river boards, and added to this the responsibility for water conservation under the 1963 Act. (The river authority for the Isle of Wight, the Isle of Wight River and Water Authority, also operates as a statutory water undertaker under the terms of a local Act, the Isle of Wight River and Water Authority Act 1964.) Two existing bodies, the Thames Conservancy (established in 1857) and the Lee Conservancy Catchment Board (which derives from the Lee Conservancy Board, established in 1868) were reconstituted and given responsibility for water conservation as from 1 April 1965. For convenience we follow the normal usage and employ the term 'river authority' to refer to all 29 bodies. The functions of river authorities constitute different aspects of river management, and we describe them individually below.

51.  The boundaries of river authority areas follow natural watersheds, and each river authority is responsible for a complete river basin or several adjoining basins. Twenty-two river authority areas are wholly in England, four wholly in Wales and three straddle the Anglo-Welsh border. Between them they cover the whole of England and Wales apart from an area of 410 square miles in and around Greater London known as the 'London

1  Department of the Environment Circular 2/70; Welsh Office Circular 116/70.
2  Nor do the new arrangements apply to water supply or river authority services.

excluded area'. Within the London excluded area certain river authority functions are not exercised, and the remainder are at present shared between the Thames Conservancy, the Kent River Authority, the Greater London Council and the Port of London Authority.

52. A river authority has between 21 and 45 members. A bare majority of these are appointed by the county councils and county borough councils in its area in proportion to their rateable value. Generally speaking the remainder are appointed by the appropriate minister because they have special knowledge of some field which is relevant to river management. The Minister of Agriculture, Fisheries and Food appoints members in respect of land drainage, fisheries and agriculture; the Secretary of State for the Environment and the Secretary of State for Wales appoint members in respect of public water supply, industry other than agriculture and in a few cases navigation. In addition the National Coal Board appoints one member to the Trent River Authority and one member to the Yorkshire Ouse and Hull River Authority; certain river authorities have members appointed by navigation or harbour authorities; and the Secretary of State for the Environment appoints a member to the Thames Conservancy to represent recreation.

53. A river authority typically has four or five chief officers: a clerk, an engineer, a treasurer, and either a fisheries officer and a pollution officer or a single officer responsible for both functions. Some of the smaller authorities share one or more chief officers with county councils.

## Water conservation

54. Under the Water Resources Act 1963 a river authority has a general duty to take whatever action is necessary to conserve, redistribute or otherwise augment the water resources of its area; to secure the proper use of these resources; or to transfer any of these resources to the area of another river authority. In practice this has boiled down to the following activities:

(i) preparing and implementing hydrometric schemes for measuring the rainfall, evaporation and river flows within its area;

(ii) investigating the water in underground strata;

(iii) surveying the water resources of its area, and the existing demand, preparing an estimate of future demand, and formulating proposals for action (whether by the river authority or by other persons) to meet future demand (the survey, known as a 'section 14' survey, has to be reviewed every seven years);

(iv) controlling abstractions of surface and underground water by means of a system of licensing;

(v) constructing and operating major conservation works.

A further activity, the determination of minimum acceptable flows for surface sources in consultation with all the interested parties, was expected at the time of the 1963 Act to assume great importance, but because the statutory provisions are insufficiently flexible no formal determinations have been made.

55. The present licensing system for abstractions of surface and underground water superseded a limited system of control for underground water which had previously been operated by the ministry. Existing abstractors were automatically entitled to a licence, subject to the payment of fees and charges (see para. 60). There is a right of appeal to the minister for anyone who is refused a licence or who is dissatisfied with the conditions attached to it. In addition to certain general exemptions, for example for domestic abstractions and many categories of agricultural abstractions, the minister has power to make an Order exempting all abstractions in a given area from licensing, and a few such Orders have been made.

56. The role of the river authority in relation to the construction and operation of works is to augment the water available in sources of supply for subsequent abstraction. Typically this means augmenting the flow in a river by discharges from a reservoir or from a pipeline transferring water from another catchment or from underground sources, techniques which are collectively known as 'river regulation'. Another technique is artificially recharging underground aquifers with water, although it is still at the experimental stage in this country. A river authority also has the power to construct a reservoir in order to enable another party to abstract water from it. It does not have the power to construct an intake for a water undertaker, or the works between the intake and the consumer such as trunk mains, treatment works and service reservoirs. Nor does it have the power to give bulk supplies of water direct to water undertakers through pipelines.

57. Prior to the 1963 Act virtually all works intended to benefit public water supply, including some works used for river regulation, were constructed either by individual undertakers or by one of the small number of bulk supply boards or joint authorities. The 1963 Act gave river authorities the power to acquire existing works used for river regulation either by agreement or compulsorily, but no transfers of this kind have taken place: one reason is that works owned by river authorities are not subject to rates and the effect of the transfer would normally reduce the rateable value of the local authority in whose area the works are situated. River authorities are also empowered to enter into an agreement with the owner of a reservoir about the manner in which it is to be operated, and it is hoped that this will enable some existing reservoirs used for other purposes to be converted to river regulation.

58. Because of the time necessary to design and obtain authorisation for schemes, no conservation works constructed by a river authority are as yet in operation. A scheme to transfer water from the Great Ouse system to regulate rivers in Essex is, however, nearing completion, as is a small barrage at the mouth of the Essex Stour. Powers have been obtained for the construction of river intakes and a storage reservoir by the Welland and Nene River Authority, and are currently being sought for several other schemes. In several cases a river authority and a water undertaker have promoted a joint Bill.

19

*Finance*

59. Up to now expenditure by river authorities on water conservation has been quite small but it is expected to increase rapidly in future. Revenue expenditure (including loan charges) has been:

| | |
|---|---|
| 1965/66 | £1,026,000 |
| 1966/67 | 1,214,000 |
| 1967/68 | 1,484,000 |
| 1968/69 | 1,843,000 |
| 1969/70 | 2,804,000 |

Source: Association of River Authorities

In 1967/8 river authorities estimated that in 1973/4 revenue expenditure would have increased to £8.8m.

60. Since 1 April 1969 expenditure on water conservation has been met by the licensed abstractors in each river authority area through a separate water resources account. They pay both a small annual licence fee and variable charges, which are calculated from the size of abstraction authorised and such factors as the quality of water and the purpose for which it is used in such a way as to reflect the significance which a licence-holder's operations have for the management of water resources: thus, other things being equal, a licence to abstract a given quantity of water for direct cooling would attract much lower charges than a licence to abstract the same quantity of water for, say, public water supply. There is provision in the 1963 Act for contributions to be made by river authorities towards the cost of works constructed by water undertakers and vice versa, but the normal expectation is that works will be financed by whichever body constructs them. There is a 50 per cent exchequer grant available towards expenditure on hydrometric schemes and investigations of underground strata but, although this is relatively important to river authorities at the moment, it will cease to be so as total expenditure increases.

*Control exercised by central government*

61. The Water Resources Board advises both river authorities and central government about water conservation. This advisory role is discussed below. In addition the payment of exchequer grant to river authorities on hydrometric schemes, investigations of underground strata and other research work is dependent upon the Board's technical assessment of an authority's proposals.

62. As noted above the minister has appellate functions under the licensing system which river authorities administer. A statement of minimum acceptable flow would be subject to the minister's confirmation. A copy of each section 14 survey has to be sent to all the ministers concerned, but it does not require their formal approval. The charges levied on abstractors by a river authority are governed by its charging scheme, which has to be approved by the minister: the current charging schemes are intended to cover the period 1969-74.

63. River authorities require loan sanction from the minister before they can borrow to finance capital expenditure, and if they require compulsory powers to carry out works these may be included in an Order made by the

minister. Through an oversight the 1963 Act did not give river authorities an indemnity from legal action in respect of discharges of water, and up to now this has meant that authorisation for conservation schemes has had to be sought through private Bills instead of through ministerial Orders. There is an amending Bill at present before Parliament which if it is passed will allow river authorities to use the ministerial Order procedure for the great bulk of future schemes. Under the terms of the amending Bill an Order authorising the discharge of water in, or the discharge of water taken from, a National Park or Area of Outstanding Natural Beauty will have to be laid before Parliament and will be subject to annulment by a resolution of either house.

## Land drainage and sea defence

64. In land drainage matters river authorities are the successors to the river boards established by the River Boards Act 1948, and through them to the catchment boards dealing solely with land drainage which were established for certain river systems under the Land Drainage Act 1930. They exercise a general supervision over land drainage within their areas; and they are directly responsible for the maintenance and improvement of those watercourses which have been designated as 'main river' and for the sea defences which protect low-lying coastal areas from inundation by the sea. Sea defence is an important feature of the work of many river authorities, particularly on the east coast.[1]

65. River authorities have a general responsibility for supervising the activities of any internal drainage boards (see para. 12) within their areas. Of the 368 internal drainage districts 69 are in fact managed directly by the river authority concerned. In the case of the others the river authority has a default power if the board fails to exercise its functions properly.

66. County borough and county district councils have limited powers under land drainage legislation to prevent flooding, or to remedy or mitigate the damage caused by flooding, from watercourses not under the direct control of the river authority. These powers are substantially the same as those of internal drainage boards. A county council may also exercise these powers at the request of a district council, or if the district council is not exercising its powers. As the river authority has an overall responsibility for supervising the drainage of its area, local authorities are required to seek its consent before undertaking drainage works.

67. River authorities and county and county borough councils have power to undertake drainage work at the request of, and at the expense of, third parties. They also have power to undertake schemes compulsorily for improving the drainage of any land in their area at the expense of the owners of the land affected.

68. Surface water run-off into rivers and streams from urban development is creating increasing difficulties for river authorities in the exercise of their land drainage functions. New towns and other large-scale building operations

1 Coastal county borough and county district councils, together with three *ad hoc* bodies, are responsible under separate legislation for 'coast protection', the protection of coastal areas which are not low-lying against erosion or encroachment. In 1968/9 capital expenditure for this purpose was £3m, of which rather more than half was met by exchequer grants.

present special problems which can often only be met by major land drainage work. More intractable problems arise from the cumulative effect of comparatively small-scale development. Local planning authorities have been made aware of the special importance of full consultation with river authorities on proposals for development which are liable to cause flooding problems; and arrangements exist, which are currently under review, for liaison to ensure that the implications of new development can be assessed before planning permission is given. But the more effectively this work is undertaken the greater the burden for river authorities. The volume of this work is increasing.

*Finance*

69. Gross expenditure (revenue expenditure plus capital expenditure) on land drainage and sea defence by river authorities, and previously by river boards, has been as follows in recent years:

| | expenditure £m | length of main river miles |
|---|---|---|
| 1955/56 | 9.7 | 15,963 |
| 1964/65 | 14.2 | 18,096 |
| 1965/66 | 14.7 | 18,061 |
| 1966/67 | 16.3 | 18,494 |
| 1967/68 | 17.4 | 18,718 |
| 1968/69 | 18.9 | 19,159 |
| 1969/70 | 20.5 | 19,212 |

Source: Association of River Authorities

70. The Ministry of Agriculture pays grants to river authorities towards the cost of approved schemes for new work or works of improvement at rates ranging from 10 per cent to 80 per cent, the actual rates varying according to an individual authority's financial resources and the volume of work it carries out. Additional grant premiums are payable towards the more costly and difficult sea defence projects. Grants at a flat rate of 50 per cent are made to internal drainage boards, and also to county and county borough councils and to river authorities in respect of schemes carried out at the request and expense of riparian owners and occupiers; grants are made to local authorities towards their own flood protection works on a differential scale ranging from 20 per cent to 50 per cent. Grant is not payable on maintenance work. There is a special grant to river authorities for flood warning systems.

71. After allowing for exchequer grants, river authorities finance their net expenditure on land drainage mainly from precepts levied on local authorities and on internal drainage boards. Five river authorities have also made use of powers under the Land Drainage Act 1961, which are available to all river authorities, to levy drainage charges on occupiers of agricultural land outside internal drainage districts.

72. Internal drainage boards finance their net expenditure from drainage rates levied on the owners and occupiers of property in their districts. Local authorities meet their expenditure on land drainage from the general rate.

**Control of pollution**

73. The River Boards Act 1948 transferred to river boards the control of river pollution previously exercised, rather ineffectively, by county borough and county district councils. The powers which river authorities inherited from river boards in 1965 had, however, been greatly strengthened by the Rivers (Prevention of Pollution) Acts 1951 and 1961, the Clean Rivers (Estuaries and Tidal Waters) Act 1960 and the Water Resources Act 1963. The Thames and Lee Conservancies have additional powers for controlling pollution contained in local Acts passed in the mid-nineteenth century.

74. Under the Rivers (Prevention of Pollution) Act 1951, the consent of the river authority is required to new discharges of trade or sewage effluent to inland waters. The 1961 Act extended this requirement to pre-1951 discharges. The river authority may refuse consent, and if it gives consent will normally attach conditions governing the quality of the effluent and other matters. The applicant may refer any disputed point to the minister. The river authority is required to review the conditions imposed from time to time. Discharges of surface water from sewerage systems are frequently polluting: some river authorities give conditional consent to such discharges, others do not regard them as requiring consent. Under the 1963 Act the consent of the river authority is required to discharges of trade or sewage effluent (or other polluting matter) to underground strata through a well, borehole or pipe. River authorities also seek to prevent pollution by means of consultations with local planning authorities.

75. Under the Clean Rivers (Estuaries and Tidal Waters) Act 1960 river authorities have a general power to control new or altered discharges in all estuaries of any significance. The minister has power to make Orders under the Rivers (Prevention of Pollution) Acts which give full control over both new and existing discharges to a given estuary; a few such Orders have been made but none in the major estuaries. All discharges to the tidal Thames, however, are controlled by the Port of London Authority under local Acts.

76. The Jeger Committee has recently recommended that control should be extended to all discharges to all estuaries (including those not covered by the 1960 Act), and to discharges to the sea within the three-mile limit. These powers would be exercised by the authorities responsible for the control of river pollution. The government is considering this recommendation.

77. In addition to their regulatory functions river authorities have power under the Water Resources Act 1963 to carry out works to make the quality of any inland water more suitable for a use for which it is required, and to take action to deal with accidental pollution.

*Finance*

78. The expenditure of river authorities on the control of pollution is almost entirely on administration and enforcement, and is therefore on a relatively small scale. In recent years gross expenditure (revenue expenditure plus capital expenditure) has been as follows:

| | |
|---|---|
| 1955/56 | £222,000 |
| 1964/65 | 389,000 |
| 1965/66 | 684,000 |
| 1966/67 | 979,000 |
| 1967/68 | 1,146,000 |
| 1968/69 | 1,227,000 |
| 1969/70 | 1,361,000 |

Source: Association of River Authorities

This expenditure is met by a precept on county and county borough councils. The expenditure of the Port of London Authority on the control of pollution is at present met from its general revenue, but it is considering seeking contributions from other authorities. Expenditure for the purposes mentioned in para. 77 is met from the water resources accounts of river authorities.

*Control exercised by central government*

79. The minister decides any matters referred to him in relation to consents to discharge. In addition treatment works constructed by sewage disposal authorities in order to comply with the terms of consents issued by river authorities require loan sanction from him (see para. 49 above). In recent years restrictions have had to be placed on less essential sewage disposal schemes as part of general restrictions on capital expenditure in the public sector, but it has been recognised that most schemes are urgently needed. The ministry has given appropriate advice to river authorities. The restrictions were withdrawn in Ministry of Housing and Local Government Circular 44/70, Welsh Office Circular 46/70, issued in June 1970. This said that priority should continue to be given to sewerage and sewage disposal schemes needed for housing, industry or for reasons of public health, to fit rivers for use as a source of water supply and to end the gross pollution of beaches; and that the criterion for schemes outside these categories should be the benefit which they would confer upon rivers or aquifers.

**Fisheries**

80. The objective of the fisheries work of river authorities is to conserve a natural resource, while at the same time permitting the legitimate exploitation of a valuable commercial resource and a very important recreational resource. The Jeger Committee estimated that there were 3m anglers in England and Wales. A survey organised by the Natural Environment Research Council has subsequently concluded that there are 2.79m anglers, and that their annual gross expenditure is in the range of £192m-£250m, an average of £70 - £90 per angler.

81. In general river authorities are responsible for maintaining, improving and developing the salmon, trout and freshwater fisheries within their areas in accordance with the Salmon and Freshwater Fisheries Acts 1923-65. Their byelaw powers allow them *inter alia* to fix or alter close seasons, to determine the nets or other instruments to be used for fishing and their manner of use, to determine minimum sizes of fish that may be taken, and generally to take steps to conserve and improve stocks. They issue licences

and determine duties for rods, nets and other fishing methods, and regulate the valuable commercial fishing for salmon and sea trout in river estuaries and off our coasts. They also administer the special pollution provisions in section 8 of the 1923 Act. Increasingly, they are becoming concerned with scientific aspects of management, and several run hatcheries for restocking. Some own fisheries. In the areas of the Thames and Lee Conservancies the major provisions of the Salmon and Freshwater Fisheries Acts are not applicable, but the Conservancies have made byelaws under local Acts which relate solely to the protection of fish in specified lengths of the main rivers.

82. Fisheries protection, and the enforcement of byelaws, statutory provisions and local Acts and Orders is carried out by fisheries officers supported by water bailiffs, many of whom are part-time or honorary.

83. In recent years the gross expenditure (revenue expenditure plus capital expenditure) on fisheries has been as follows: —

| | |
|---|---|
| 1955/56 | £165,000 |
| 1964/65 | 400,000 |
| 1965/66 | 437,000 |
| 1966/67 | 542,000 |
| 1967/68 | 577,000 |
| 1968/69 | 769,000 |
| 1969/70 | 771,000 |

Source: Association of River Authorities

The income derives mainly from fishing licences. A number of authorities still have powers to assess privately owned fisheries and to levy what the 1923 Act calls 'a contribution' on them; but a report awaiting implementation recommends that this latter power, which is little used, should now cease, and this recommendation has been accepted by the government. The balance of income stems from a precept on county and county borough councils. Although authorities generally set out to defray as much of their expenditure as possible from fisheries income, in practice this is rarely if ever capable of achievement today. In total, between one-quarter and one-third of income is from the precept.

**Navigation and recreation**

84. The Thames Conservancy is the navigation authority for the non-tidal Thames (above Teddington). The Department of the Environment believes that another twelve river authorities have statutory responsibilities for navigation over a total of about 500 miles of river and canal, although it emphasises that its information may not be up-to-date or complete. In some instances the stretch involved is tidal and in some other instances the river authority is seeking to extinguish the navigation rights.

85. The gross expenditure of the Thames Conservancy on navigation in 1969/70 was £732,000. Two other river authorities showed income and expenditure on navigation separately in their accounts: they spent £37,052, of which the Kent River Authority accounted for £36,777.

86. In addition to their powers in relation to navigation and in relation to fisheries, which are both nowadays important for recreational purposes, river authorities have general powers to make byelaws to regulate the recreational use of non-tidal waters where this appears to be necessary or expedient for the purposes of their other functions. There are certain exceptions, however, including inland waters under the control of a navigation authority other than the river authority. If a river authority has made byelaws for an inland water, or if it owns or manages a reservoir itself, it may provide facilities for recreation. Such facilities are required to be financially self-supporting.

87. Under section 101 of the 1963 Act river authorities (together with the Water Resources Board and the relevant ministers) are required, in exercising their functions under the Act, to have regard to the desirability of preserving natural beauty; of conserving flora, fauna and geological or physiographical features of special interest; of protecting buildings and other objects of architectural or historic interest; and of preserving public rights of access.

88. Under the Countryside Act 1968 statutory water undertakers have a parallel power to that of river authorities to provide recreational facilities at reservoirs or waterways which they own or manage.

89. The British Waterways Board administers about 2,000 miles of canal and river navigation in England, Wales and Scotland. Among the major rivers for which it is the navigation authority are the Lee, Severn and Trent. Its waterways are divided under the terms of the Transport Act 1968 into three categories: commercial waterways (about 340 miles); cruising waterways, which are intended to cater for recreation and amenity associated with cruising and fishing (about 1,100 miles); and remainder waterways, which are to be dealt with in the most economical manner possible, having regard to public health, amenity and safety (about 600 miles). In 1969 the total expenditure of the Board on its waterways was £3,724,000, of which £2,442,000 was spent on cruising and remainder waterways.

## THE WATER RESOURCES BOARD

90. The Water Resources Board was established in 1964 under the Water Resources Act 1963 as a national agency for data collection, research and planning. The Board consists of eight members appointed jointly by the Secretary of State for the Environment and the Secretary of State for Wales. Apart from the Chairman and the Director they are appointed for their knowledge of a particular field relevant to water resources: one of the members is required by the Act to have special knowledge of conditions in Wales. Members are paid but apart from the Director they are part-time.

91. There is a non-statutory Welsh Committee of the Board. This is chaired by the Welsh member of the Board and at present consists of a second Board member, the chairmen of the seven Welsh and Anglo-Welsh river authorities, and five other members with experience and knowledge of particular Welsh interests.

92. The Board has a staff of about 160 and an annual expenditure of about £1.5m, of which about £300,000 is research grants to river authorities. The expenditure is met by the exchequer and the staff are civil servants. Its offices are at Reading. Internally the staff are organised into six divisions: Research Division, Resources Division and four planning divisions.

93. The Board's field of work is water conservation in the sense in which that term was used above in describing the work of river authorities. Within this field its central activity is planning. In 1966 it produced a report on the development of water resources in South East England to the year 2000. A parallel report on the North was published in February 1970 and one on Wales and the Midlands will follow later this year. These reports have been based on the reports of Technical Working Parties chaired by the Board and consisting of representatives of the river authorities and water undertakers in that particular area. Together the Board's three reports cover the whole of England and Wales, apart from South West England. Alongside these regional studies, feasibility studies are in progress of the potential for storage in Morecambe Bay and the Dee Estuary (the latter by the Dee Crossing Steering Committee, on which the Board is represented); and desk studies have been carried out of the potential in the Wash and in the Solway Firth. A report has also been published on the costs of desalination.

94. At the same time the Board is setting up a national system for collecting water resources data to form a better basis for planning. It provides technical assistance to river authorities in relation to hydrometric schemes and the investigation of underground strata; and it can give directions to them on these matters. It also controls the payment of exchequer grant for these purposes. It is directly responsible for the processing of the data collected and for the publication of the Surface Water Year Book and the Ground Water Year Book. The Board's research activities are related to its planning and data collection functions. It carries out research itself and it also promotes and co-ordinates research by river authorities and other bodies.

95. The Board has taken an active part in the negotiations over the implementation of its reports, and it is required to monitor the progress that is made in this direction. In essence, however, it is an advisory body, giving advice in two directions, to river authorities and to central government. It does not have any power to construct and operate works itself, except for research purposes. In the course of its duties it has found it necessary to take account of water quality, flood alleviation, land drainage, fisheries and recreation, all aspects of managing water resources which on a strict interpretation are outside its terms of reference, and on which it has largely had to rely on outside advice. It has on occasions set up *ad hoc* committees, for example a Fisheries Advisory Committee, to meet this requirement.

## CENTRAL GOVERNMENT

96. The responsibility for the different aspects of water in England and Wales is divided between three ministers. The Secretary of State for the

Environment, as successor to the Minister of Housing and Local Government, is responsible for water conservation, water supply, sewerage and sewage disposal, pollution control and coast protection in England; as successor to the Minister of Transport, he is responsible for navigation in England and Wales; and he also has a general responsibility for the protection of the environment and for sport and recreation. The Secretary of State for Wales is responsible for water conservation, water supply, sewerage and sewage disposal, pollution control and coast protection in Wales. The Minister of Agriculture, Fisheries and Food is responsible for land drainage (including sea defence) and fisheries in England and Wales. Certain functions in relation to river authorities are exercised jointly by two or three ministers.

97. Under the Water Act 1945 and the Water Resources Act 1963 the Secretary of State for the Environment and the Secretary of State for Wales have a joint duty:

(a) to promote the conservation and proper use of water resources and the provision of water supplies in England and Wales and to secure the effective execution by water undertakers, under their control and direction, of a national policy relating to water;

(b) In formulating a national policy relating to water, to include such measures as they may consider necessary or expedient for augmenting the water resources of areas in England and Wales, for redistributing water resources in any such area or for transferring water resources from one such area to another;

(c) to secure that, under their control and direction, the national policy will be effectively executed by the river authorities and the Water Resources Board, as well as by statutory water undertakers, in so far as that policy relates to matters falling within the functions of those bodies respectively.

The Water Resources Board is responsible for advising the ministers with respect to the discharge of these duties.

98. The Directorate of Engineering of the Department of the Environment advises the ministers and officials of the Department and of the Welsh Office on the merits and priorities of proposals for capital expenditure. It gives technical guidance to water undertakers, sewerage and sewage disposal authorities, and river authorities; and has provided members for the large number of committees and working parties appointed by the minister to consider technical aspects of water services. Its inspectors conduct inquiries and hearings in connection with the ministers' functions. The Directorate includes chemists, public health engineers and other specialists who give advice to the departments and to other bodies, including the Water Resources Board, on questions of water quality.

99. The Directorate is at present carrying out a River Pollution Survey with the co-operation of river authorities, sewage disposal authorities and the Confederation of British Industry. The aim of this survey is to establish in some detail the degree of pollution in tidal and non-tidal rivers, and to assess the cost of restoring them to a satisfactory condition and main-

taining them in that condition. The data are now being processed and a report will be published. A Steering Committee on Water Quality representing the various interested parties has been established to promote and co-ordinate studies of particular problems of water quality and studies of water quality in selected catchment areas. The Department have subsequently established working groups in collaboration with the river authorities concerned to consider problems of water quality in the Great Ouse, Lee and Thames areas; and others may follow.

100. The principal powers of central government in relation to particular services have been referred to above in the section dealing with each service. Considered generally, these powers may be divided into four groups:

   (i)  appellate functions: for example, deciding appeals and references against the decisions of an authority, and confirming compulsory purchase orders and byelaws;

  (ii)  negative controls in relation to the construction of works: agreeing or refusing to grant loan sanction, or make works Orders under the Water Acts;

 (iii)  powers of direction which require an authority to take positive action, and powers of default: the only general power of direction is in connection with the water conservation functions of river authorities, although there are specific powers on other matters. Default provisions are common form but in practice have virtually never been used;

 (iv)  payment of exchequer grant: the availability of a specific exchequer grant does not ensure that an authority will undertake a given project, but it makes it more likely.

101. Having given a brief description of the present system of organisation we now go on, in chapters 2 and 3, to consider the problems facing it and the way in which it is working.

## 2. THE PLANNING OF RESOURCES

### THE NEED FOR NATIONAL PLANNING

102. The Proudman Committee, to which we referred in the preface, was appointed by the Central Advisory Water Committee in October 1955 to consider the extent to which the demand for water was increasing and the problems involved in meeting those demands. Its final report, published in 1962, showed that on the basis of the returns provided for the ministry by statutory water undertakers the consumption of water had been increasing at an average rate of 2.4 per cent a year over the period 1955-60. It concluded that 'Firm longer-term forecasts are not available but there seems to be no obvious limit to the growth in demand for water from statutory water undertakers, both to meet increased domestic consumption consequent upon rising social standards and to serve the growing demands of industry.' The Water Resources Board have subsequently stated that by the end of the century the present output of water conservation works will

need to be doubled, an estimate which if anything presupposes some reduction in the present rate of increase in demand.

103.  Meeting this increasing demand constitutes a major problem. Exploitable water in England and Wales is scarcer than is often thought; the average amount available per head of population, about 850 gallons a day, is among the lowest in Europe, only Belgium, East Germany and Malta having less.[1] Moreover rainfall is heaviest in the mountains of the north and west, away from the areas where industry and population are concentrated.  The Proudman Committee considered that precipitation was sufficient to provide adequate supplies.  But the demand cannot be met except by a further development of the means of conservation.  And since in all districts the relatively inexpensive local sources of supply have already been intensively developed, it is inevitable that in future increasing quantities of water must be moved over long distances and radically new plans examined.

104.  Although much of England is short of water, Scotland is not.  But the main deficiency areas in England are in the south east, and even for the deficiency areas in the north of England the high cost of transmission links means that the transfer of water from Scotland has no obvious advantages over the further conservation of water in England, at least for several decades.

105.  From time to time the desalination of sea water is advocated.  On the information available to the Committee the widespread use of desalination in this country is remote, although in parts of the South East desalination plants might find an important place as a supplementary source during the last two decades of this century.  In any event the use of desalination does not introduce any further complexities into the planning procedures required, and for the purpose of our particular investigation it can therefore be disregarded.

106.  One of the recommendations of the Proudman Committee was the creation of 'comprehensive new authorities' to manage the water resources of river basins as a whole: they envisaged that as well as taking over the responsibilities that were then being exercised by river boards for land drainage, fisheries and the control of pollution the new authorities would also be charged with a positive duty to conserve, and ensure the best use of, all the water resources of their areas.  The majority of the Committee recommended that these authorities should be of a new type with a small and compact membership of, say, 10-15, some of whom might be full-time. A minority of the Committee thought they should be formed by reconstituting the existing river boards, which had an average membership of 28. The recommendation to create 'comprehensive new authorities' was implemented by the establishment of 29 river authorities; but the government accepted the view of the minority of the Committee about their composition and their average membership is the same as that of the river boards, without any full-time members.

1 United Nations, Economic Commission for Europe. Trends in water resources use and development in the E.C.E. region (ST/ECE/Water/1) p.4, table 1. 1970.

107. The Proudman Committee also recommended the establishment of a central authority to promote an active policy for the conservation and proper use of the country's water resources. This was achieved by the setting up of the Water Resources Board. River authorities have to consult the Board about the preparation of their section 14 surveys, and the proposals for action they put forward have to include proposals for giving effect to any notice or advice that they have received from the Board. The Board in its turn works closely with river authorities and also with statutory water undertakers.

108. With the help of the river authorities and statutory water undertakers, the Board has looked at the period up to the end of the century and has come to the conclusion that it is necessary to study the resources of England and Wales as a whole. In its current studies it has divided the country into three regions (omitting the South West of England): the North, the South East, and Wales and the Midlands. It came to the conclusion that the resources in each of these regions could only be developed at a reasonable cost in terms of resources and land use if there were substantial transfers of water from one river basin to another and from one river authority area to another, and considerable use of river regulation. Moreover, the most efficient solution may well involve switching particular works to serve different areas at different times. For these reasons it is no longer possible to plan the use of water resources effectively except over very extensive areas. By the year 2000 it seems likely that about one quarter of all public water supplies will be conveyed across the boundaries of the present river authority areas. In the extreme cases of the Lee Conservancy and the Mersey and Weaver River Authority the proportion of external supplies is forecast to increase to 50 per cent and 70 per cent respectively.

109. Even the three regions which the Board has studied are not necessarily self-sufficient in water resources, and there will almost certainly have to be substantial transfers of water into the South East and into Lincolnshire, and/or the building of estuarine storage in the Wash, by the end of the century. It may well turn out to be desirable to provide storage in Morecambe Bay and the Dee Estuary, not only to satisfy the needs of south Lancashire and Yorkshire, but to provide an exportable surplus of water for the Midlands and further south. It is therefore necessary not only to consider regional water plans but a national plan as well, covering the whole of England and Wales. It is in fact the Board's intention, when the report on Wales and the Midlands has been published, to draw together the three regional studies, and the other studies it has published, plus certain supplementary studies and the results of further investigations, into a national study which will provide a comprehensive framework for the future management of water resources in England and Wales. This national study is expected to be completed in 1972.

110. **For all the above reasons we conclude that the future development of water resources can best be planned over England and Wales as a whole.**

THE IMPORTANCE OF WATER QUALITY

111. We have included as appendix 2 to our report a note on water quality

prepared for us by the Directorate of Engineering of the Department of the Environment. For further information we are again able to refer the reader to the recent report of the Jeger Committee.

112. In the north, where water undertakers initially found ample supplies of good upland water available, the middle and lower reaches of many rivers were allowed to become so polluted by domestic sewage and industrial effluents during the nineteenth century that their waters could only be used for industrial purposes, including a very large usage for cooling. In the south east, on the other hand, the Thames was a major source of water for domestic purposes, and the Thames Conservancy was set up in the mid-nineteenth century to improve the state of the river, which was giving rise to frequent epidemics, and conserve the navigation. The cleaning up of the river was a slow process because sewage treatment methods had to be developed and installed before the dumping of crude sewage could be eliminated, but by the turn of the century the non-tidal Thames was reasonably clean. Despite a big increase in population since the turn of the century and the large-scale development of modern industry, an insistence on high (and where necessary very high) standards of effluent and the operation of weirs in such a way as to increase the river's capacity for self-purification have led to a further improvement in its condition.

113. Today about 180 mgd of sewage effluent and about 42 mgd of trade effluent are discharged into the non-tidal Thames; and the Metropolitan Water Board draws from it over 300 mgd, two-thirds of London's water supply. This situation involves a high degree of reuse of water.

114. Events on the Lee followed a similar course. The Lee is only 57 miles long, has a population in its catchment area of about 2 million, and receives sewage effluent from that population and its associated industry. Nevertheless, it is able to provide about a fifth of London's water supply. Whereas the average dilution of treated sewage effluent by river water is 4:1 upstream of the first of the Metropolitan Water Board's two intakes, and 3.5:1 upstream of the second (and larger) intake, the dilution at the second intake is often as low as 1:1 during summer flow conditions.

115. It has now been realised that the fast increasing consumption of water, domestic and industrial, will make imperative a much greater reuse of water in nearly all parts of the country.

116. Given a free choice, regardless of cost, most water undertakers required to supply potable water from surface sources would probably prefer to go to the upper parts of catchments where the water would be generally unpolluted, but a number of factors are combining to make such sources more and more difficult to find and exploit economically. The cheapest and nearest sources were usually developed first and, as demand has grown, so has the cost of exploiting upland sources and transporting the water. Furthermore, a section of public opinion has become very hostile to the location of reservoirs in upland areas. We discuss the difficulties over the building of new reservoirs in appendix 3. Their relevance in the present context is that they have helped to create a demand that water should be abstracted from a river in its lower reaches. This does not resolve the problem of storage

during dry flow conditions and, if reservoirs are not provided in upland areas, there will be a need for much larger areas of land to be available for pumped storage reservoirs on the banks of the lower reaches. It does, however, increase the problems of quality control. Water undertakers will with increasing frequency have to draw their additional supplies from stretches of river which contain substantial proportions of effluents from sewage works and from industry and may be liable to sporadic pollution from toxic substances.

117. In the south east in particular, public water supplies will depend materially and increasingly on the reuse of effluents discharged into rivers. For example, it is estimated that by the end of the century effluents discharged to the Thames upstream of Teddington will make a contribution of about 240 mgd to public water supplies. In some river basins reuse will involve the recirculation of treated sewage effluents to consumers through downstream intakes. In other cases water containing significant quantities of effluent will be transferred from one river system to another. Clearly the effective promotion of a policy of reuse will involve the detailed study, and the positive planning, of the location and character of discharges throughout a river basin. And the parameters traditionally used in controlling discharges may need to be modified or supplemented.

118. An extreme instance of the question of what to do about pollution is provided by the Trent. The Trent is the third largest river in England and Wales and has a potential yield comparable to that of a major barrage scheme; but at present it is heavily polluted by sewage and industrial effluents and therefore unsuitable for public water supply. Indeed there is a fundamental conflict between existing and potential users of this major river. Some wish to see it carry away their effluents; others wish to develop it as a major source of supply. A committee convened by the Ministry of Housing and Local Government and the Water Resources Board in 1967, and including representatives of the Trent River Authority and the Water Pollution Research Laboratory, concluded that only a major research study embracing all the interests involved (including industry, recreation and fisheries) would enable the right decisions to be made about the future use of the river. This study is due to be completed in mid-1971 at a total cost of about £500,000.

119. The increased importance of water quality will clearly have to be reflected in the planning procedures that are followed. **The necessity for the reuse of large quantities of water demands that there must be a single, comprehensive water management plan for every river basin, which includes water reclamation.**

### 3. WEAKNESSES IN THE PRESENT SYSTEM

### THE OBSTACLES TO SUCCESS

120. In the preceding chapter we have given a brief account of the long-term problems facing the water services in England and Wales. The main issues are the quantity, the quality and the cost of raw water supplies, and the interplay of these factors with the other aspects of water. None of the needs

can be considered in isolation from the others. The task of coping with the increased use of water is a formidable one but, in the light of present knowledge and experience to date, there appears to be no technical reason why it should not be undertaken successfully. Our remit is to make recommendations which will enable this to be done in a way that is publicly acceptable, and with the greatest economy in effort, time, money, land use and social disturbance.

121. The technological advance in recent years has brought into prominence the administrative problems involved in the more comprehensive management of water. The obstacles to success can be classified under three headings: defects in the existing legislation; inadequacy on the part of some or other of the various operating units; and structural defects in the way in which water functions are organised and co-ordinated, leading to serious conflicts of interests.

## LEGISLATIVE DEFECTS

122. The 1963 Act was a major step forward, and the new bodies which were set up have made considerable progress with the tasks which were assigned to them. We note that river authorities have been handicapped by certain defects in the Act. For example they have to apply for a ministerial Order before they can investigate a possible site for a reservoir, merely to authorise the investigation; and if the application is opposed a public inquiry has to be held. On the other hand, because of the oversight referred to in para. 63, a ministerial Order following a public inquiry is not in practice sufficient authorisation for the construction of a reservoir or other water conservation scheme, and they have had to promote private Bills. Neither these points nor certain other limitations on the present powers of river authorities in the field of water conservation to which our attention was drawn are of fundamental importance from the organisational point of view, and we have not therefore examined them in detail. We have assumed that where necessary amending legislation will be passed as soon as possible, and we have already noted that a government Bill dealing with the most urgent point is at present before Parliament.

123. A more fundamental defect in the Act was that in 1963 the importance of the quality of water in rivers, streams and underground strata and its relationship to resource management were not fully appreciated. As a result, insufficient attention was given to the roles that the Water Resources Board and the river authorities should play in taking positive action to improve the quality of effluents. It is generally considered that the effluent from a sewage works should as a minimum maintain the standard recommended by the Royal Commission on Sewage Disposal over 60 years ago para. 43). A higher standard may need to be achieved where the 8 times dilution factor is impossible or where the discharge is on a large scale and the river is used for a purpose requiring high-quality water. In these circumstances, it may be necessary to impose further limitations, for example on the ammonia content of discharges and, where a discharge contains trade effluents, on other parameters. The river authority specifies the appropriate standard when it gives its consent to a discharge. But, although

many sewage works are models of efficiency, a considerable proportion do not in practice meet the consent conditions of the relevant river authority.

124. River authorities can prosecute local authorities and other dischargers who fail to comply with the terms of a consent, but prosecution is regarded as a last resort and local authorities in particular have scarcely ever been prosecuted. A riparian owner may take civil action against a discharger who infringes his riparian rights (whether or not the discharger is complying with the terms of a consent) and there have been some successful actions of this kind. Such an action may lead to the installation of additional treatment plant but equally it may lead merely to the discharge of the same effluent at a different point, where is may even cause more damage. Much has been written about the shortcomings of sewage works, and, particularly in view of the recent publication of the Jeger Report, we do not intend to say any more. The Jeger Committee recommended various amendments to the existing legislation, and the government are considering its recommendations. We are convinced, however, as was the Jeger Committee, that a policy of tightening the existing system of control, supported by detailed improvements in legislation, will not bring about the changes that are essential within the available time-scale. Much more far-reaching measures are needed, which we discuss later.

## THE ADEQUACY OF THE OPERATING UNITS

125. Neither 'efficiency' (performing a task in the most economical way) nor 'effectiveness' (answering fully a particular purpose) is necessarily correlated with size, but it is undoubtedly true that very small operating units find it difficult to acquire staff of the right calibre and in the required numbers to cover their present duties adequately. As a result, they risk being ineffective. Should there, then, be a reduction in the number of separate units in any of the fields we are concerned with?

### River authorities

126. If we disregard the Isle of Wight, the areas covered by river authorities vary between 350,000 acres (Lee Conservancy) and 3,352,000 acres (Yorkshire Ouse and Hull). There seemed to be a widespread view in the evidence submitted to us that the number of river authorities should be reduced. Some river authorities shared this view, others argued strongly against any reduction. Some drew a distinction in this context between the different functions performed by a river authority. We came to the conclusion that the optimum number of river authorities needed to be considered in conjunction with other questions, and we do this in chapter 5.

### Water undertakings

127. As we pointed out in para. 19, the number of water undertakings has been substantially reduced since 1945 but they still amount to about 200. It was generally agreed by the British Waterworks Association and the individual water undertakers who gave evidence to us that the process of re-grouping, which has slowed down in recent years, ought to continue in order to secure a more efficient deployment of staff and resources. They suggested

that the ideal size for a water undertaking depended on such factors as the density of population and the geography of a particular area. Where a figure for the eventual number of undertakings was mentioned in the evidence submitted to us it was 100 or less.

128. In their evidence, the Institution of Water Engineers stated that in rural areas water undertakings should serve a population of 100,000 or more, and in urban areas at least 300,000 and preferably up to 750,000. They also said that they saw no reason for efficiency to fall off even in undertakings serving 2 or 3 million people.

129. In view of this we feel that the ultimate number of seperate operating units for water supply should probably be significantly lower than 100 and when, for illustrative purposes, we talk of the desirable number of units we therefore use the figure 50.

## Sewage disposal units

130. The present sewage disposal authorities constitute about 1,300 separate operating units, managing some 5,000 treatment works. This excessive fragmentation is a major cause of weakness, and of the poor performance referred to in para. 123, and we feel that a drastic reduction in the number of separate operating units is required. As with water undertakings, we are not in a position to specify what amalgamations should take place, or what the ultimate number and areas of the operating units should be. But for illustrative purposes we assume that the operating units will eventually number about 50.

## STRUCTURAL DEFECTS IN ORGANISATION

131. The present division of responsibilities produces conflicts of interest between the various authorities. These conflicts often have the advantage that the various bodies have to argue their cases cogently in order to secure agreement, but there is the serious disadvantage that it may not be possible to achieve the best overall solution. Indeed the conflicts may preclude any agreement being reached at all, so that the eventual solution has to be imposed from above, by central government. Some of the most important examples of the conflicts to which we refer are the following.

## Inflexibility in the use of existing resources

132. The existing source works used by water undertakers are vested either in them or in one of the small number of bulk supply boards. The better utilisation of existing sources can give very considerable benefits and delay the need for the construction of further source works. Three ways in which this can be done are by converting direct supply reservoirs to river regulating reservoirs; by making conjunctive use of several sources of different types (for example surface sources and underground sources); and by switching a source from supplying one area to supplying another, or from one user to another. These are all measures which individual water undertakers can and do take with their own sources. But they are difficult to achieve at present where several undertakers are involved because the

agreement of each undertaker is required; and the effect may be to increase the costs of one undertaker in the intersts of reducing costs over the area as a whole, or to alter the quality of the water supplied to a particular area.

133. The position over the redeployment of bulk transmission networks is if anything more difficult than that over redeployment of sources. The river authority has no power to acquire bulk transmission networks or to control their method of operation. The bulk supplies between water undertakers are in some important cases governed by rigid terms laid down in a local Act, perhaps without provision for alteration, or in long-term agreements. This makes it difficult to adjust them to meet changing circumstances. Moreover, conscious of their statutory obligations, undertakers have tended (with the consent of the minister) to obtain reservations on particular sources well in advance of their actual requirements, again without necessarily any provision for alteration.

**Divided responsibility for new sources**

134. The obligation to supply water for domestic purposes, and therefore the responsibility to procure adequate supplies, lies upon the water under-takers under the Water Act 1945. The legal obligation is to provide a whole-some and continuous supply, but there is a social obligation to supply water which is palatable. There is also a legal obligation, if supplies are sufficient, to make water available for those other purposes, such as industry and trade, on which the life and prosperity of the community depend, and this water should, so far as is possible, be of the right characteristics to meet industrial needs.

135. Under the Water Resources Act 1963, a water undertaker may not abstract water from a source except under licence from the river authority. It is the duty of the river authority to take such action as they consider necessary or expedient for 'conserving, redistributing or otherwise aug-menting water resources in their area', but there is no legal obligation on them to find more water. The only obligation is that when carrying out section 14 surveys and dealing with licensing matters 'a river authority shall have particular regard to the duty of any relevant statutory water under-takers to provide supplies of water' (section 103). Even this obligation specifically excludes industrial and trade supplies.

136. It is true that some river authorities are accepting their responsibilities towards water undertakers to a degree which is beyond criticism, but there are other river authorities who, being short of water, find this difficult. Some river authorities also feel that they have been handicapped by the defects in legislation referred to in para. 122 and by the hostility of a section of public opinion to the construction of reservoirs to which we refer in appendix 3. It is not that water undertakers and river authorities do not try to resolve the problems which arise but that, looking at them from different stand-points, they may disagree as to what should be done. Some instances of the difficulties which can occur are: —

    (i) the river authority may prefer to license one source on wider grounds of water conservation, whereas the water undertaker may prefer another source on financial grounds;

(ii) the river authority may wish the water undertaker to use a source which, in the latter's eyes, is too polluted for safety, or has undesirable characteristics in relation to use by industry, or is more expensive to treat than some other possible source;

(iii) opinions may differ as to the quantity of water an undertaker should be licensed to take from a new source;

(iv) the river authority may not feel able to issue a licence until it has itself promoted some river regulation or other scheme, or until it has carried out further investigations, whereas the water undertaker judges that the need is too urgent to await these events in this connection it was pointed out to us that, from the point of view of the water undertaker, the planning machinery established under the 1963 Act and the lengthy consultations to which it inevitably gives rise have themselves been a source of delay);

(v) the 1963 Act provides for water conservation schemes to be financed, either wholly or in part, by all the licensed abstractors in a river authority's area through its water resources account. This creates scope for disagreement over the financing of a scheme, particularly where an undertaker finds that he is both contributing to the cost of a scheme to benefit other undertakers and meeting the whole cost of his own source works.

137. The resolution of these difficulties is made all the harder when the water must come from a river authority area which is remote from the water undertaking concerned. In some cases where an undertaker is in urgent need of more water he may feel there is a risk of his defaulting on his legal obligations to supply water.

138. The question of whether a given source is suitable for public supply may be particularly difficult to resolve. The decision depends not only on the known quality of the water, but upon an assessment of the risks involved in using that supply, in which assessment safety must be paramount.

139. The difficulties outlined above are becoming causes of great concern to water undertakers. They have a statutory duty to supply water when required to do so, but they do not control the sources. If they want to challenge a decision by a river authority they have to make a formal appeal or reference to the minister. This is a major defect in the present situation, and we feel that no structure will be satisfactory unless it satisfies the following criterion: **If a body is under a statutory obligation to supply water, then either it must itself have the powers to enable it to meet this obligation, or there must be another body which has a statutory obligation to make water available to it.**

## The promotion of joint or national schemes

140. Even though the work of the river authorities and the Water Resources Board is resulting in the formulation of a national plan for the augmentation of resources, the fact that the individual schemes contained in the plan would normally involve several river authorities means that it is diffi-

cult to promote them. The Water Resources Board has no executive powers. And the minister cannot stand fully behind some regional joint scheme because at a later stage he may well have to hold an impartial inquiry into whether that scheme should be permitted to proceed or not.

141. Much depends, therefore, on the various authorities and undertakers getting together and agreeing to promote a joint scheme. This is illustrated by the discussions that are now taking place over the implementation of the Water Resources Board's report on the North. Clearly in some cases such negotiations will be successful and a joint scheme will go ahead. There is already evidence, however, that they may also be difficult and time-consuming, and that there is no adequate machinery at present for resolving the conflicts that arise. The best that can be done is for the minister and the Water Resources Board to play an informal co-ordinating role. Where differences of view arise concerning the amount each party should pay, these may prove particularly intractable and may effectively delay the promotion of a scheme for a prolonged period, even though only two undertakers or authorities of the same kind are involved. This is important because schemes inevitably take time to design and build, and time is short if we are to meet the needs of the late seventies. Moreover the distinction between schemes carried out and financed by river authorities and schemes carried out and financed by water undertakers is a somewhat arbitrary one. The 1963 Act provided for special contributions between river authorities and water undertakers (para. 60), but the ministry and the Water Resources Board dislike such contributions in normal circumstances, on the grounds that they give a particular water undertaker a vested interest in a particular source, and create obstacles to its future redeployment. Although this reasoning appears sound, the absence of such contributions could increase the arbitrariness of the distinction between river authority schemes and water undertakers' schemes.

142. We have already referred in paras. 132-3 to the difficulties of varying the manner in which existing works are utilised. Similar problems of inflexibility could arise with new schemes. Indeed they would be increasingly severe. Whether or not a very large project is economic depends on the degree of utilisation that can be achieved in the early years. It may be necessary as a temporary measure to arrange for a particular project to serve a larger area, or a different area, to that which it will serve eventually; and when the project is constructed the period of time before the change-over may not be known.

143. Situations of this kind are in fact envisaged in the report on the North, and under the present system of organisation a number of separate bodies would be involved. In these circumstances difficulties could be expected to occur over the financing of the project, especially the unremunerative expenditure in the early years.

144. The difficulties would become even greater of course with a large-scale delivery network within which yields had to be switched about a number of times. The Water Resources Board are exploring the possibility of an integrated network of this kind for the central area of South East England: this area covers three river authority areas and parts of two others, and at

present contains 46 water undertakings and a bulk supply board. Discussions are in progress between the five river authorities involved about the implementation of this proposal. Under the present system of organisation an *ad hoc* body would be necessary to build and operate the network. This would be a body of quite a new type and its establishment would present considerable problems.

## Conflicts of interest in regard to water reclamation

145. We have already referred to the lack of observance of the consent conditions concerning sewage effluents, and to the difficulties of reducing the pollution in rivers by having recourse to legal proceedings. The basic reason is the conflict of interest between those who discharge effluents into a river and those who abstract water from that river or use it in other ways below the points of discharge. For a variety of reasons, which are well known but no single one of which is dominant, expenditure on sewage treatment is, in all too many cases, kept to the minimum that the discharger can get away with. Expenditure by the discharger will probably only benefit those who abstract water or use it in other ways further downstream, and therefore the reluctance to incur more than the minimum expenditure is in some ways understandable. Water reclamation is a problem for, and a benefit to, the whole of a river basin, but at present sewage treatment is regarded as an entirely local matter and paid for out of the local rates. Another implication of this is that large volumes of effluent are discharged direct to the sea, or to tidal estuaries, when they might have been discharged at a point inland and reused. Certainly in the absence of any system for equating the costs and benefits of water reclamation the progress in improving the quality of water in our rivers will be unacceptably slow.

## Wider conflicts

146. In addition to the conflicts of interest we have discussed above between the authorities responsible for water, there are also certain wider conflicts which extend into other spheres and must also be taken into account. One class of such conflicts, which has recently proved to be of some importance, arises when proposals to use land for water purposes are thought to conflict with amenity or with existing uses. The most obvious example is the use of land for reservoirs, which we discuss in appendix 3. But disputes may also arise over proposals to use the land for sewage disposal works and, as such works become larger and land in urban areas becomes scarcer, the number of disputes of this kind is likely to increase.

147. Another class of conflicts arises in the opposite way, when other activities interfere or threaten to interfere with water functions. The use of a river for water supply, for example, may place limitations on the kind of industry that should be established in its catchment area. Alternatively, a requirement to improve its effluent might in extreme cases drive a firm out of business and create unemployment. On the land drainage side, the river authority will want to restrict development within the flood plain of a river. These wider conflicts are not ones that we are directly concerned with, but they are of at least equal importance and we have therefore had to bear them in mind.

148. Under the present system of organisation, then, the number of occasions on which conflicts of interest arise between the various water authorities is increasing, and the mechanisms for resolving these conflicts are inadequate. As a result the present system seems to depend to an undesirable extent on the intervention of central government, whether informally or through the use of a formal appeals procedure by one of the parties. Clearly an appeals procedure may be a very necessary safeguard, especially for private abstractors and dischargers. Clearly, too, there are some decisions which (like those mentioned in paras. 146-7) have such widespread implications in other fields that central government necessarily becomes involved. But for every dispute between public bodies to have to be referred to Whitehall is slow, cumbersome and frustrating. We have already said that we believe it is essential that a comprehensive water management plan must be drawn up for every river basin. **Once such plans have been agreed, the system of organisation and the financial arrangements must be such as to permit their implementation.** The relationship between the various bodies in the water field must be changed so as to satisfy these criteria, and we analyse in the following chapters how this might be done.

## 4. THE NEED FOR EFFECTIVE CO-ORDINATION

### THE NATIONAL PLAN

149. In the two preceding chapters we have set out the case for the comprehensive management of our water resources, and we have argued that it is a corollary of this that the system of organisation and the financial arrangements must be such as to permit both the formulation of overall plans and their subsequent implementation. In the present chapter we discuss in general terms how planning and co-ordination should be carried out in future in the water field, and how this would differ from the present arrangements. Then, in subsequent chapters, we go on to discuss the alternative systems of organisation that can be devised to ensure that the necessary planning and co-ordination are undertaken.

150. In chapter 2 we showed that the future development of water resources can best be planned over England and Wales as a whole. This fact has already been accepted. The Water Resources Board is well established as a national planning body and an independent source of advice for central government and river authorities. With the publication later this year of the Wales and Midlands study the Board's three major planning studies will be complete. As we have said, the Board then intends to produce a national study which will incorporate the regional studies, and this will form in effect a national plan for the period up to the end of the century. The assumption is that this would subsequently be revised at relatively frequent intervals, and that these revisions would increasingly benefit from the work of local planning bodies (that is, in the present system of organisation, the river authorities).

151. The scope of national planning, however, needs to be widened to bring in water quality as well as quantity. Hitherto the Board's studies have been

primarily concerned with methods of increasing the quantities of water available, and this has determined the composition of its present staff. This is a reflection of the fact that at the time when it was established the significance of water quality was not sufficiently appreciated. As time has gone on, however, the Board has become increasingly involved in the consideration of water quality. For example, the hydrometric schemes operated by river authorities under its supervision have been broadened to cover measurements of water quality; and it has taken a leading part in promoting the comprehensive study of the river Trent (para. 118), in which the problem of water quality is central.

152. The Water Resources Board will therefore need to be expanded in future to form a 'National Water Authority'. This will employ experts in a wider range of disciplines than the present Board, so that all the relevant aspects of water can be taken fully into account in the national plan, and so that the future national authority can provide the same technical leadership in the planning of water quality as the present Board provides in its existing field of work. At the same time, a section will be needed within the national authority to examine in more detail the economic and financial aspects of water plans.

153. The purpose of a national plan is to provide a strategy within which more detailed planning, and subsequently executive action, can proceed. There must be adequate opportunity for public debate about the issues involved. But once the strategy has been agreed, it must be regarded as a firm general commitment of government policy, unless and until the periodic reviews show that changing circumstances have brought about the need for substantial modifications. We suggest that these objectives could be achieved if the work of the national authority were to form the basis for a Green Paper on national water policy which the appropriate ministers would present to parliament, and which could then be debated. While this paper would concentrate on the broad principles which the government considered should be followed in water planning, it would also have to deal with the largest individual projects, for example barrage projects and others of comparable significance.

## THE ACTION PROGRAMME

154. In order to ensure that the works required to implement the national plan are constructed as and when they are needed, there must in addition be action programmes based on the national plan, but covering a shorter period, say, five years. An action programme will distinguish between the individual years within the five-year period and will be in two parts. The first part will contain the works that have to be constructed during that five-year period. It will show for each project the date when construction will start, the length of the construction period and the value of the work to be carried out in each year. The second part will contain those works which are expected to be constructed in subsequent five-year periods. For these latter projects the action programme will indicate the timetable that needs to be followed in obtaining the necessary authorisations (planning permission, compulsory purchase orders, etc.), and in other preparatory work

such as drawing up detailed designs, if their construction is not to be delayed. The action programme would be rolled forward annually.

155. Some further explanation is needed of what we mean by an action programme, and why we regard it as important. The aggregate value of the projects in the first part of the action programme would represent the amount that central government had decided, in the light of the economic situation and increases in the demand for water, should be spent on water services in that particular five-year period. The choice of the projects to be included in the programme, and thus the distribution of this amount, would be made by the bodies responsible for water functions in such a way as to produce the best overall result. The starting-point for their choice would be the analysis and appraisals contained in the long-term plan, and these would be supplemented by more up-to-date and detailed information. Some of the projects which were candidates for inclusion in the action programme would be interdependent, and these linkages would have to be taken into account. Once the contents of the programme had been settled, all the bodies covered by it would be under an obligation to act in accordance with it. Clearly there would have to be consultations with the relevant ministers about the content of action programmes, but we discuss that aspect in paras. 226-9.

156. Eventually we envisage that the first part of the action programme will contain only projects for which all the necessary authorisations have already been secured before the beginning of the five-year period. At the moment this would be impossible because there is a backlog in the construction of works to meet the situation created by the increased use of water: by the time authorisation has been obtained for a particular project, it is usually already overdue. Clearly, however, the objective must be to end this state of affairs, and we believe that the various changes in organisation we are envisaging will make that possible.

157. This brings us to the question of the body that should be responsible for drawing up the action programmes, and supervising and monitoring their implementation. The possibility that these tasks, as well as the drawing up of the national plan, might be undertaken centrally by the national authority is unattractive because it would be very difficult to implement and would lead to an undesirable degree of centralisation. Moreover, although both the national plan and the action programmes will cover all the relevant aspects of water, we think that the latter ought to cover a wider range of projects in terms of size than a national plan of the kind we envisage could sensibly cover. They ought, for example, to cover the exploitation of local sources of underground water and the construction of at least the more important sewage disposal works. These considerations lead us to the following conclusion: **Action programmes must be drawn up on a regional basis, covering all the separate bodies carrying out water functions in the region. There must be a body in each region with the statutory duty of compiling action programmes for the region, and with staff of the right skills and experience to enable it to do so.** We designate this body by the title of the Regional Water Authority.

158. The term 'region', however, can have a number of different meanings,

and we must therefore explain more precisely what we mean by it in this context. On account of the growing interdependence of the quantity and quality of water it is desirable for planning purposes that a region should be as large as possible. On the other hand, if it is too large, the managerial problems become too difficult to handle. The size of a region must therefore be such as to achieve a reasonable compromise between these two requirements.

159. As regards planning, the following seem to be the most important factors that must be taken into account. Because we are concerned with water functions, a region must be a river basin or a grouping of river basins. It must cover an area which is reasonably self-sufficient in water resources; it should not be an aim of policy to make individual regions entirely self-sufficient because that would lose the benefits that could otherwise be gained from national planning, but a region should not be predominantly dependent, either now or in the foreseeable future, on imports of water from other areas. Regard must be paid to the future pattern of transfers so as to keep to a minimum the number of regional authorities involved in each major transmission network. A region should be large enough to support, and keep fully employed, a planning team containing the necessary disciplines. Finally, because in any system of organisation the distribution of costs will be determined in some measure by the areas chosen, the regions should be large enough to achieve a reasonable equalisation of costs in relation to major works and therefore avoid extremes which are the result of past actions.

160. It is less easy to propound any rules about the desirable size of a region as regards managerial functions. But, in principle, managerial functions should be decentralised as far as possible, consistent with the economical use of scarce manpower; and as a rough generalisation one can say that a 'region' ought to be the smallest area which satisfies the criteria for effective planning.

161. It is not part of our task to recommend how many regions there should be, or to attempt to fix their boundaries. But it seems likely that the use of the criteria we have outlined above would lead to the conclusion that there should be not less than six regions in England and Wales and not more than fifteen. For illustrative purposes we have printed in appendix 5 two maps showing possible boundaries for such regions if there were respectively seven and thirteen of them; and, whenever in discussing general principles it is necessary to quote a single figure for the number of regions, we use the median figure of 10. In considering particular systems of organisation, it will, however, sometimes be necessary to be more precise than this (see for example paras. 216 and 219).

## THE REGIONAL PLAN

162. As well as the national plan and the regional action programmes, it will also be necessary for the Regional Water Authority to draw up a regional water management plan covering a longer period than five years. This might be a relatively straightforward interpolation between the national plan and the regional action programmes; or it might require further studies

to be carried out, partly by the national authority and partly by the Regional Water Authority. Like the national plan, it would be essentially a strategic plan, but it would go into greater detail than would be appropriate or possible in the national plan. The plan for a given region would incorporate any of the specific projects in the national plan that were located in that region. It would also apply to that region the general policies in the national plan about the use of water and the improvement of water quality and spell out their implications in terms of specific projects, for example, the new works needed to achieve a given improvement in river conditions. Regional plans of this kind would be a development of, and would supersede, the surveys which river authorities are now required to carry out in consultation with the Water Resources Board under section 14 of the 1693 Act. They would differ from the section 14 surveys, however, in covering not only the development of new sources of water and the redeployment of existing sources, but also the standards of water quality to be aimed at and the methods of achieving them. They would also deal with the economic and financial aspects of their proposals. They might cover the same time-scale as the section 14 surveys, that is, twenty to thirty years. They would be the 'water management plans' we envisaged in chapter 2 (para. 119), and the action programmes would provide the means of implementing them.

163. The regional plan would be drawn up on the basis of estimates of future population and industrial activity for the region as a whole, and of the distribution of that population and activity within the region. Broadly speaking, the assumption hitherto has been that the provision of water and sewage disposal are service functions which should adapt themselves to a pattern of development shaped by other factors: they should not themselves determine the pattern of development. This assumption needs to be qualified in certain respects, in that there are certain cases in which water considerations ought to be decisive. We have in mind such questions as the location of industries which use very large quantities of water or produce particularly difficult effluents, or proposals for development within the flood plain of a river. But the broad assumption contained in the second sentence of this paragraph is correct and it should continue to be made in future. The Regional Water Authority would be placed under an obligation to have regard to the structure plans of the relevant local authorities in performing its own functions.

164. The long-term regional plans will have to be flexible so that they can be adapted successfully to changing circumstances. The fact that they will be based upon land-use plans which will themselves have to be altered from time to time to meet changing circumstances reinforces this point. They should be published, in order to give an opportunity for public debate on them, but they will not override the normal procedures for sanctioning abstractions or discharges, or for authorising the construction of new works.

## PLANNING AND CO-ORDINATION AS A DISTINCT FUNCTION

165. We regard the function of compiling action programmes for a given region and supervising and monitoring their implementation as an extremely important one. It is also to a large extent a new function. The nearest

equivalent is the work on water resources planning at present carried out by river authorities. But the work on the regional planning and co-ordinating bodies, as we envisage it, would go a good deal further than that at present undertaken by river authorities. It would give a more central place to quality considerations, and the evaluation of the economic and financial aspects of water management. And the regional planning and co-ordinating body will have a direct and positive responsibility for ensuring that the action programme is implemented. In view of the scale and complexity of the activities involved, its task will be one of considerable difficulty.

166. In each region therefore we can distinguish four basic functions: water supply, sewage disposal and river management, which to some extent merges into the fourth function of planning and co-ordination. All four functions have to be carried out efficiently if we are to make the best use of our water resources. This does not necessarily entail that there ought to be four different types of body in each region, one type to perform each function. There might be advantages in combining several functions within a single body, provided it was clearly recognised that that body was performing several quite different functions, and provided also that its management structure was such that it could deal efficiently with all these functions. This is a question we go on to discuss in the next chapter, but there is one consideration which follows directly from the nature of the system of financial planning that the action programmes constitute and places a significant limitation on the forms or organisation that can be adopted.

167. At present proposals for sewage disposal works formulated by a local authority (which are the great majority) have to compete for a share of that authority's capital investment programme with projects which it wishes to carry out in connection with its functions. Whether or not they are implemented, therefore, depends on the relative priorities that the authority attaches to sewage disposal and to its other functions. Under the system we have described, a proposal for a sewage disposal works will be competing not against local government projects in general but only against other proposals for major works in the water field in that particular region, including for example, river purification works and reservoirs. This reflects the interdependence which already exists, and will increasingly exist, between the different aspects of water. The inclusion of a project for a sewage disposal works in an action programme will mean that it is an integral part of the best obtainable package for that region in that programme period. This system would be completely ineffective if that project could subsequently be considered by a local authority in a different context, and according to different criteria, and as a result be rejected or postponed. This does not mean that sewage disposal cannot in our view continue to be a function of local authorities. What it does mean is that, if sewage disposal were to continue to be a function of local authorities, they would have to accept certain limitations on their freedom of action in relation to it, and in particular their freedom to make the final decision on how much should be invested in it.

## CONCLUSION

168. The result of the foregoing considerations can be summed up as follows.

The strategic plans drawn up at the national level must be extended to cover all the relevant aspects of water management. They must conform to and not dictate the general development plans of the country; and they should be reported to Parliament and, if desired, debated so as to ensure that the concepts involved have general public acceptance. These long-term strategic plans are not and cannot be detailed plans covering the budgets of all the bodies responsible for river management, water supply and sewage disposal in the country. It is, however, essential that the budgets of these bodies should be properly co-ordinated and integrated, and, on account of their complex interrelationships and the wide variety of local circumstances, this co-ordination should be carried out on a regional basis, a region being briefly defined as a river basin or grouping of river basins which is sufficiently large to be reasonably self-sufficient in water resources. This regional co-ordination of all water functions is largely a new feature in water management and we firmly believe that it is an essential one. We believe that the number of regions, as defined in this chapter, should be of the order of ten and that there must be a planning and co-ordinating body in each region, which we designate by the title of the Regional Water Authority. In each region there are then four distinct functions to be carried out, namely, the three executive functions of river management, water supply and sewage disposal, and the supervisory function of planning and co-ordination. We devote the next chapter to an analysis of the relationship of these four functions, and the nature and constitution of the bodies which should be responsible for carrying them out.

## 5. THE ALTERNATIVE SYSTEMS OF ORGANISATION

### THE TWO APPROACHES

169. In chapter 3 we arrived at the conclusion that the number of separate operating units in the fields of water supply and sewage disposal should be substantially reduced, and we have assumed that the reduction will be to about 50 in each case (paras. 127-30). In chapter 4 we concluded that action programmes covering these function and those of river management need to be co-ordinated on a regional basis, and that the desirable number of regions for this purpose is of the order of ten. In each region there would be a planning and co-ordinating body, which we have designated the Regional Water Authority.[1] It follows, purely as an arithmetical average, that a typical RWA would be responsible for co-ordinating the activities of three of the existing river authorities, five of the new and larger water supply units, and five of the new and larger sewage disposal units. (These average figures are for illustrative purposes only. As can be seen from the maps in appendix 5, the number of the existing river authorities in a particular region might be as low as one or as high as six).[1]

170. We now have to analyse in more detail the roles of the different units in each region (on average 14 in number: the RWA and 13 other units) and the way in which they should be interrelated.

1 In this chapter we have abbreviated 'Regional Water Authority' to 'RWA'.

171. With four functions to be dealt with (water supply, sewage disposal, river management, and planning and co-ordination), there are many forms of organisation possible. The obvious extremes are (1) to have all four functions carried out by one body, namely, the RWA itself; and (2) to have each function carried out by a separate type of body. For convenience of reference, we shall refer to the first form of organisation as one based on multi-purpose authorities and to the second form of organisation as one based on single-purpose authorities. In the first case, there would be ten RWAs in England and Wales, which would be multi-purpose bodies. In the second case, there would be ten RWAs which would be single-purpose planning and co-ordinating bodies, together with 29 river authorities, 50 bodies responsible for water supply and 50 bodies responible for sewage disposal.

172. Neither of these forms of organisation obtains at the present moment, because the existing river authorities are multi-purpose bodies which have a limited planning and supervisory role combined with the executive functions of river management. There are also other forms of organisation which are intermediate between the multi-purpose and strictly single-purpose forms. We shall have to refer to all these intermediate organisations in our considerations, but with different degrees of emphasis. However, all systems of organisation which contain single-purpose authorities have strong similarities to one another, and they differ fundamentally from a system based on multi-purpose authorities. We therefore deal first with the extreme cases, and go on to consider intermediate cases later.

## A SYSTEM OF ORGANISATION BASED ON
## MULTI-PURPOSE AUTHORITIES

173. As we have seen in chapter 3, a major source of difficulty in the present situation is conflicts of interest between separate statutory bodies, and, in particular, conflicts concerning who should own and pay for physical assets. One way of lessening these conflicts would be to transfer all the relevant assets and all the relevant functions to a single body, the RWA.

174. In this system of organisation each RWA would be an independent statutory body. It would replace the river authorities and water undertakers in its area and take over their assets. It would also replace, and take over the assets of, any bulk supply board or joint water authority within its area. It would take over the ownership and operation of treatment works and trunk and off-site sewers from local authorities and joint sewerage boards. It might also take over the canals in its area, at least those which have a potential importance as sources of water, as aqueducts, or as methods of effluent disposal. The responsibility for public on-site sewers, however, would remain with local authorities.[1] Internal drainage boards would continue as at present.

175. The central objective of an RWA of this type would be to act as a public utility, providing or disposing of water and making economic charges for doing so. (The provision of water is here thought of as covering both

1 For the terms 'off-site sewer' and 'on-site sewer' see para. 37

the present functions of water undertakers and the functions of the present river authorities in the field of water conservation. On the disposal side we shall use the term 'sewage disposal' to cover the treatment of domestic sewage and trade effluents, together with responsibility for trunk and off-site sewers.) Each RWA would be obliged to satisfy financial criteria laid down from time to time by the minister, such as a requirement to break even or to achieve a prescribed degree of self-financing. At the same time, it would be under a statutory obligation to maintain and improve the state of the rivers in its area in accordance with the national plan; and it would retain regulatory functions under the control of pollution legislation, for example in relation to private discharges of effluent direct to streams. It would be subject to the general law on such matters as land-use planning. As far as possible it would be subject to commercial criteria, but where there was any risk that it might abuse its powers, there would be special safeguards, for example in the form of a right of appeal to the minister, and these are discussed below.

176. The authority itself would be a body of 10-15 members: these could be appointed by the relevant ministers or, if it were thought desirable, a proportion of them could be appointed by the major local authorities. The chairman would be appointed by the ministers on the basis of his proven ability in guiding complex organisations. The day-to-day management would be in the hands of a number of full-time chief officers under a full-time chief executive. The chief executive would be a member of the authority, and possibly some of the other chief officers as well. The remaining members of the authority, including the chairman, would be paid on a part-time basis.

177. The RWA would have a number of operating divisions; the form of these would be a matter of internal management for the authority to decide and might be changed from time to time. Initially there would probably be three operating divisions, responsible respectively for river management, water supply and sewage disposal. But the authority would be quite free to adopt a different split, for example between planning, design and construction, and operation.

178. Each of the operating divisions would be in the charge of one of the chief officers; and in addition there would be a sufficient number of chief officers to cover all the central functions such as planning and co-ordination, law, finance, contracts, budgetary control and the regulation of direct discharges. The exact division of work between the regional headquarters and the operating divisions would be an internal matter for the authority to decide. There is no reason why the operating divisions should not have a considerable degree of independence within the framework of a proper system of costing and budgetary control.

179. In additions to performing its essential functions as the legal owner of the physical assets and the co-ordinating body for the operating divisions, the authority might find it economically desirable to arrange for certain services (for example, computing or laboratory services) to be provided centrally on behalf of the operating divisions.

180. The operating divisions would be further split up into a number of local units, each in the charge of an area manager who would have consider-

able freedom and responsibility in dealing with local matters and local bodies. If the operating divisions dealt respectively with river management, water supply and sewage disposal, then the units in the river management division would be based initially on the areas of the present river authorities, and those in the other two divisions would correspond to the 50 separate operating units we envisaged for each of these services above. The units would not, however, have any separate legal existence, and their boundaries or size could be altered at will when it seemed desirable. It might prove advantageous for some of the day-to-day work on the central functions to be carried out locally by the units in an appropriate division, for example, enforcement work on direct discharges.

## Finance

181. It is envisaged that the total amount paid in charges by each category of consumer for each of the services provided by the RWA would be as nearly as possible equal to the total costs incurred by the RWA in providing that service to that category of consumer. Included in the total costs would be the appropriate proportion of central administrative costs, together with an equitable share of the cost of common central services. Capital charges would be assessed in the light of the financial criteria laid down by the minister (para. 175). To illustrate the application of this principle, those consumers who obtained their water by direct abstraction would contribute towards the costs of assessing, controlling and augmenting water resources. These costs might be apportioned by means of a formula similar to the present charging schemes, so that the amount each consumer paid would initially be roughly comparable to the amount he had previously paid to the river authority in abstraction charges under the 1963 Act, but the payments would now be regarded as direct payments for a service. Those consumers, on the other hand, who used piped water would contribute both to these costs and to the costs of treatment and distribution. In both cases the rates of charge would be standardised throughout the area of the RWA.

182. Although it follows from the principle stated at the beginning of para. 181 that the charges made to each category of consumer for providing water would be based on the cost of providing water, and the charges for disposal on the cost of disposal, the expenditure for both purposes would be met from a single General Water Fund, and the individual consumer would be presented with a single bill in which the two charges were consolidated. This would reflect the fact that, from the point of view of the RWA, providing and disposing of water within a river basin (or group of related river basins) would be complementary activities.

183. The method of raising revenue suggested above is a simple extension of the methods already used for water supply, water conservation and trade effluent disposal to public sewers, although in the last case the present charges are normally discretionary. It differs in principle, however, from the method used at present for sewage disposal (including trade effluent disposal where no special charge is made), which is financed from the general rate as a public health service. One effect of changing to a system of charges would be to remove the assistance which the exchequer at present gives

towards the cost of sewage disposal through the Rate Support Grant (para. 47). Another effect might well be a shift in the burden of financing sewage disposal as between different categories of consumer. There are considerable difficulties, however, in predicting the precise effects of such a change and we have therefore included as appendix 4 to our report a note prepared for us by the Department of the Environment on 'Exchequer grants and the financing of sewerage and sewage disposal', which discusses these points.

184. There is an alternative method of financing sewage disposal in a system of multi-purpose authorities which would achieve many of the same advantages as the method just described but involve fewer uncertainties, and this is as follows. The RWA would make charges to firms for collecting and dealing with trade effluents. For collecting and dealing with domestic sewage, it would make charges to the local authorities from whose areas it received the sewage according to an acceptable formula. Any disputes about the application of the formula would be determined by an arbitrator appointed by the minister. (It is essential that consent to discharge trade effluents to a sewer should be given by the RWA and not by the local authority, because of the close relationship between the composition of such effluents and the operation of its works, and it is logical that the RWA should also handle trade effluent charges.) The principles governing rates of charge would be standardised throughout the area of the RWA. Local authorities would obtain the money to meet the RWA's charges from ratepayers generally through the general rate. And their expenditure for this purpose would presumably be taken into account in calculating whatever form of exchequer assistance was currently available to local authorities.

185. A further advantage of this alternative method of financing is that, although a local authority would have no direct control over the activities of the RWA, it could constitute a more effective watchdog on its efficiency than the individual consumer. If the method suggested earlier, a single fund and a single bill sent directly to each consumer to cover both the provision and the disposal of water, was thought to be a desirable objective, the alternative method just outlined could nevertheless be useful as a transitional stage.

186. The cost of treating direct discharges of effluent to the prescribed standard would continue to be met by the discharger, but if the RWA in its regulatory capacity required a discharger to produce an unusually high standard of effluent it would be given the power to make a grant towards the cost of treatment.

187. The RWA would continue to levy charges for fishing licences. The remainder of its expenditure on fisheries, and its expenditure on regulating private discharges of effluent, might be financed out of the General Water Fund, as this would add less than one per cent to the annual expenditure from the fund. The expenditure of the RWA on land drainage could continue to be met from precepts and exchequer grants. Internal drainage boards would finance their activities in the same ways as at present.

188. As we implied in chapter 4, many of the RWAs will not be entirely self-sufficient in water resources and will have to import water from the

areas of other RWAs. In a system of multi-purpose authorities we envisage that this would be achieved through the sale of water by one RWA to another, as in the bulk supply agreements between the present water undertakers. Undoubtedly difficulties would arise in considering schemes which affected several regions. The importance which such difficulties assumed would depend on the number of RWAs established, and on the role taken by the national water authority. We discuss these matters in chapter 6.

## Public accountability

189. 'Public accountability' is not a well defined term and it means different things to different people. In the present context we take it to mean that the ministers would be accountable to Parliament for the large sums of public money invested in water functions, and for the general running of the bodies concerned; and that the RWAs would have to be accountable to the ministers in such a way as to allow the ministers to discharge their own responsibilities to Parliament. The question with which we are concerned therefore is in what ways the RWAs ought to be accountable to the ministers, and this question has several distinct aspects corresponding to the different kinds of function the RWAs would perform. The principal aspects appear to be accountability over regulatory or quasi-regulatory decisions; accountability over the fixing of tariffs; and accountability over operational decisions. These aspects are dealt with individually below. We disregard general controls such as land-use planning legislation to which the RWA would be subject in the same way as other bodies, and deal only with controls which would be specific to the water field.

190. First there are the regulatory or quasi-regulatory functions of the RWA. Its function in relation to direct discharges would be purely regulatory: discharges of effluent would require its consent, and it would prescribe the standards that they must attain. As it would be acting in a regulatory capacity, the existing right of appeal to the minister against refusal of consent to discharge, or the terms in which consent is given, would be preserved.

191. Although in the case of the provision of water the RWA's function would be to perform a service, it would differ from, say, an electricity undertaker or the present statutory water undertakers in the nature of its monopoly: to obtain water, whether by piped supply or by direct abstraction, the consumer would have to go through a transaction with the RWA. To meet this situation the RWA would be placed under statutory obligations to make supplies of water available to legitimate users either by pipe or for direct abstraction. Clearly there would be cases in which it would be unreasonable to provide the desired quantity of water, or unreasonable to give the consumer a choice about the method. An analogous problem already arises with the obligation on water undertakers to supply water for non-domestic purposes, and a similar solution would be adopted: the RWA would be given a right of refusal in certain specified circumstances, and the consumer would be able to refer any dispute to the minister or to an arbitrator appointed by the minister. The presumption would be that those users who hold abstraction licences under the 1963 Act would be entitled

to continue to obtain water by direct abstraction, although there would have to be procedures, corresponding to those which exist at present, for reviewing these entitlements and the quantities involved. Certain categories of user, for example people wanting water for their own domestic use, would be entitled to obtain it by direct abstraction independently of the RWA: the categories would be based on those exempt from licensing under the 1963 Act, and they might well be extended by raising the exemption limit for very small abstractions.

192. In deciding whether or not it ought to refuse to provide water for a given applicant, the RWA would have to take into account the requirements of its other functions, including land drainage, navigation and fisheries. If it were not felt that general statutory obligations would be sufficient to ensure that it did so, the present concept of acceptable flows (para. 54) might be retained. In that case the statements of minimum acceptable flows would be incorporated in the regional plan.

193. If it were thought desirable to have further safeguards to ensure that the RWA's decisions were equitable to private abstractors and dischargers, a procedure might be adopted like that used at present for the grant of abstraction licences to river authorities. For example, discharges made by the RWA itself would be brought within the system of consents to discharge which would in any case exist for private dischargers. When the RWA wanted to make a new discharge or alter one of its existing discharges, it would notify the minister, who would have the power to call in the case for his own decision: if he did not do so, he would be deemed to have given the RWA the necessary consent. If necessary, a similar procedure could also be used for the RWA's own abstractions.

194. In the case of tariffs, the national water authority would be responsible for giving advice to the ministers on the principles on which tariffs should be based and their structure, and where appropriate this might form the basis for statutory regulations governing the form of tariffs. The RWAs would submit proposals for new tariffs to the ministers at intervals, specifying maximum rates of charge. A proposed tariff would be examined by the minister to ensure that its structure was equitable and the maximum rates of charge were justified in the light of the RWA's estimates of future expenditure under the relevant headings. If there were objections to it, the minister would hold a public inquiry before deciding whether to approve or reject it.

195. There would also need to be a procedure for raising, and a means of remedying, complaints against the RWA by individual consumers. And, subject to the government's general policies on consumer protection, there would seem to be advantage in establishing channels for the direct expression of particular consumer viewpoints. We envisage therefore that there would be several consultative councils in each RWA area which would between them cover all the services it provided. In the case of the provision and disposal of water, the area covered by a consultative council would be the whole of the region although there might be separate councils for different categories of consumer, for example, domestic consumers and industrial consumers. In the case of other services which are more local

in character, such as navigation and fisheries, consultative councils might cover smaller areas such as a single river basin or a particular stretch of river.

196. Another idea which was put to us in evidence and which we think would deserve further consideration as a means of dealing with complaints is a Special Inspectorate or Water Commission. This body would be appointed by the ministers and would be empowered to investigate complaints and, if they were found to be justified, bring them to the attention of the relevant minister. Such an Inspectorate might exist alongside a network of consultative councils, fulfilling a complementary role.

## SYSTEMS OF ORGANISATION BASED ON SINGLE-PURPOSE AUTHORITIES

197. As we stated at the beginnnig of this chapter, a system of multi-purpose authorities differs fundamentally from a system based on single-purpose authorities. We now turn to look at the extreme case of systems based on single-purpose authorities, the case in which each of the four functions we have identified (water supply, sewage disposal, river management, and planning and co-ordination) is performed by a separate type of body. In order to distinguish it from other systems of organisation based on single-purpose authorities which we discuss later, we refer to it as 'System A'.

### System A

198. The objective of a thoroughgoing single-purpose structure is to leave as many as possible of the executive (i.e. operating) decisions to the operating bodies, whilst reserving general planning and co-ordination to the RWA. Thus there would continue to be water undertakers with, broadly speaking, the same functions and obligations as at present. There would continue to be sewage disposal authorities with, broadly speaking, the same functions and obligations as at present. There would continue to be river authorities responsible for land drainage, water conservation, fisheries, the control of pollution and, in some cases, navigation.

199. In particular, river authorities would continue to be responsible for the construction, ownership and operation of major water conservation schemes. In this context major schemes would include substantial works wholly or mainly for the purpose of river regulation, works for the artificial recharge of aquifers on which many different abstractors depend, and strategic transmission aqueducts. The division of responsibility for works between river authorities and water undertakers would therefore be similar to the present *de facto* situation described in para. 56, although some of the restrictions which have proved to be illogical on the activities of river authorities, for example the inability of a river authority to give bulk supplies to water undertakers by pipeline, would be removed. The planning functions at present exercised by river authorities in drawing up section 14 surveys would, however, be very substantially altered and widened, and would be taken over by the RWA. The obligation of ensuring that water

was made available to meet the needs of water undertakers and (within practical limitations) other abstractors would therefore lie with the RWA, and the river authority would be purely an executive agency.

200. There is a diagram of System A in appendix 6 and a table showing the distribution of functions between the different types of authority is at the end of this chapter. In both cases a comparison can be made with the other possible systems based on single-purpose authorities which we discuss later.

201. In reducing the number of water undertakers to about 50, the same practice would be followed as hitherto, that is to say, the area of supply and the form of new undertakings would be decided on a pragmatic basis according to local circumstances and the pattern of sources and distribution networks, and taking into account the total system of which they would be part. This would perpetuate the present pattern, in that some undertakings would be owned by companies, others by indivdual local authorities and others by joint boards of local authorities, although the proportions might differ. The companies would be answerable to their shareholders, with the local authorities in their area and the minister safeguarding the interests of consumers, and the other undertakings would be answerable indirectly to the electors in the areas of the controlling local authorities.

202. A similar practice would have to be followed in setting up larger sewage disposal units. Because natural catchment areas do not usually coincide with local government boundaries, most of the units would probably be controlled by joint boards of local authorities, but where there was a good match between boundaries they would be controlled by individual local authorities. In either case, they would be answerable indirectly to the electors in their area. It is envisaged that the responsibilities of the sewage disposal unit would extend to trade effluent control and to at least the trunk sewers.

203. Because of the special importance of water supply and disposal to industry, the joint boards and local authority committees controlling water undertakings and sewage disposal units would have a minority of outside members appointed, preferably at the local level, to represent those industries in the area which take public supplies of water or discharge trade effluents to public sewers. These appointments would also ensure that these bodies included people with knowledge and experience of the problems of industrial management and co-ordination. (This is already the case with water companies, at least some of whose directors are normally drawn from industry.)

204. River authorities would be constituted in the same way as at present: a bare majority of their members would be indirectly elected through the major local authorities, and the remainder would be appointed by the relevant ministers because they had specialised knowledge which was relevant to the functions of the authority.

205. The question of public accountability would be dealt with along the same lines as those described for multi-purpose authorities in paras. 189-96 but, because there would be greater opportunity for public debate on

the decisions of the individual bodies, the safeguards would not necessarily need to be so elaborate. The existing statutory safeguards in relation to the activities of the various types of body would continue, including general safeguards such as land-use planning legislation. They would include the submission to the minister of proposals to increase the maximum charges for water supply and the controls over the finances of water companies.

206. The RWA would be a new type of body, and the question of its constitution has to be considered in relation to its functions. One consideration is that it will be required to formulate regional plans and action programmes which will minimise the conflicts of interest between the operating bodies. If this were the only consideration, it would imply that the RWA should be made up of representatives of the operating bodies in order to reduce the chances of conflicts occurring between them and the RWA. It will, however, not merely be a co-ordinating committee: it is there to ensure that any conflicts of interest that do arise between the other bodies, and would otherwise threaten the implementation of the agreed regional and national policies, are resolved; and it will have positive powers for this purpose. In other words it may have difficult decisions to make, and unless it is appropriately constituted for that task and able to appreciate the consequences of its decisions, the effective decisions will tend to be made by the officers. This carries two implications. Firstly, the membership of the RWA should be small, and certainly not more than 15. And secondly, at least some of its members should be appointed specifically for their knowledge of water matters or of the problems of co-ordinating complex enterprises.

207. In combination, these considerations seem to point to an authority of not more than 15 members with a bare majority of its members (that is, not more than 8) appointed by the relevant river authorities, water undertakers and sewage disposal authorities. Since, apart from water companies, all three types of body would be dominated by local authorities, this would link the RWA closely with the local authorities in its area. The remaining members would be appointed by the relevant ministers for their special knowledge of water matters or of organisational problems. The chairmanship represents a special difficulty. The RWA is bound to have to make unpopular decisions which involve overruling operating bodies in the interests of the common good (although the final decision will be made by the minister, see para. 226). It must not only be capable of, but must also be seen to be capable of, taking such decisions. The difficulty might be met if the chairman was appointed by the members of the authority but the appointment was subject to the approval of the relevant ministers. If, however, it was thought that this might result in a conflict of loyalties, the chairman could be appointed by the ministers on the basis of his proven ability in guiding complex organisations. In either case, he would be paid on a part-time basis.

**Financial considerations**

208. As we pointed out in chapter 3, many of the difficulties which have to be overcome are concerned with finding equitable solutions to the financial

problems which arise when there are conflicting interests between two or more bodies in the water field, whether they are river authorities, water undertakers or sewage disposal authorities. Financial arrangements as such do not come within our terms of reference, but a discussion of the advantages and disadvantages of the various systems of organisation we are considering cannot be divorced from the financial arrangements which it would be logical and reasonable to associate with each system.

209. It is obvious that any arrangement for spreading costs over a number of the present operating units helps to solve the financial problems. Indeed, this is one of the principal reasons why we feel that the number of water undertakers and sewage disposal authorities should be substantially reduced. At the moment the charging schemes of river authorities spread the costs of a major conservation scheme over all the abstractors in the river authority area, and the degree of equalisation achieved in this way would be increased if the number of river authorities were to be reduced. The question whether there should be further equalisation of costs between the various statutory bodies which would exist after the process of reorganisation has been completed raises much more complex issues. A particular question is who should pay for the measures necessary to bring those effluents which are at present of poor quality up to the Royal Commission standard. Ought these costs to be borne by the dischargers concerned, or by those further down the river who will benefit from the improvement in water quality?

210. We have examined a number of schemes for the spreading of particular costs to meet this and other problems, but they all seem likely either to be ineffective or to involve an erosion of the independence of the separate statutory bodies. This negative conclusion is not meant to rule out payments being made by one body to another if the second body is called upon to undertake special actions, the benefits of which will accrue mainly to others; for example, we envisage that river authorities would be given the power to make a grant to a sewage disposal authority or other discharger if the circumstances of a particular river required the latter's effluent to be of a standard higher than the Royal Commission standard. The cost of these grants would be met by abstractors through the charging scheme and would therefore be spread over a considerable area. But, apart from such special circumstances, we envisage that the general financial arrangements in a system of single-purpose authorities would be very similar to those which obtain at the moment and they would therefore be as follows.

211. Water undertakers would meet their expenditure from water rates and charges as at present. Sewage disposal authorities would meet their expenditure from trade effluent charges and the general rate or (if they were joint boards) from trade effluent charges and a precept. River authorities would meet their expenditure on water conservation (including the special grants mentioned in para. 210) through charging schemes. They would meet their expenditure on land drainage from exchequer grants and precepts; their expenditure on fisheries from licence fees and a precept; and their expenditure on the control of pollution from a precept.

212. The financing of water supply and conservation projects affecting several statutory bodies, whether they were in the same region or not, would be dealt with by setting up separate schemes as at present. The RWA's own expenditure would be relatively small in System A and would be met by appropriate contributions from the other bodies.

## Alternative systems of organisation based on single-purpose authorities

213. As we made clear above, the two systems of organisation which we have so far described are not the only ones possible. There are other systems of organisation which are intermediate in character, in the sense that they would involve giving two or more (but not all four) of the basic functions to the same authority, while leaving the others to be performed by single-purpose authorities. The more important of these intermediate solutions, which are worth examining as candidates for the future system of organisation, are as follows:

    (1)   To make river authorities responsible for sewage disposal.

    (2)   To have a single statutory body responsible for both water supply and sewage disposal in a given area.

    (3)   To give the central function of planning and co-ordination, as we have described it, to river authorities.

    (4)   To divide the operational functions of river authorities into two, and to give some of these operational functions to RWAs.

214. During the early part of our deliberations we gave particular attention to the first two of the solutions referred to in para. 213 but we came to the general conclusion that the arguments in their favour would, on the whole, point to multi-purpose RWAs being even more advantageous. We did not, therefore, feel that we ought to investigate them as deeply as we have analysed the other solutions.

215. The third proposal in para. 213 is of a different nature to the first two because in principle it only differs from the present form of organisation in extending the existing regulatory and planning powers of river authorities into the more far-reaching functions of planning and co-ordination as we have described them in chapter 4. We shall refer to it as 'System B'. It differs from a thoroughgoing single-purpose form of organisation in that its aim is to build upon and enhance the present multi-purpose nature of river authorities and not to split off the enlarged function of planning and co-ordination to another body. The remaining proposal in para. 213 is described in more detail in paras. 219-23. It is a possible variant because river authorities have a variety of operational functions. We shall refer to it as 'System C'.

## System B

216. Although in principle a system in which river authorities are reconstituted as RWAs is very similar to the present one, which was described fully in chapter 1, there would be important differences. In the first place, sewage disposal authorities would be reorganised in exactly the same way

as in System A. In the second place, most of the present river authorities are too small to fill the role of RWAs, for which our criteria are firstly that they should be reasonably self-sufficient in water resources, and secondly that they should be able to support a sophisticated planning function. In order to satisfy these criteria and at the same time retain local interest in land drainage, fisheries, and navigation and recreation it would be necessary to reduce the number of river authorities by about half.

217. A general description of the new river authorities and their functions would then be as follows:

(1) River authorities would be reduced to about fifteen in number and would be renamed Regional Water Authorities.

(2) The membership of the RWAs would, like that of the present river authorities, vary between about 20 and about 45. In each case a bare majority of the members would be appointed by the local authorities in the region, and the rest would consist of individuals appointed by ministers. The chairman would be appointed by the members but the appointment would be subject to the approval of the relevant ministers: he would be paid on a part-time basis.

(3) The RWA would have the following functions: —

(i) The duties prescribed in the Water Resources Act 1963 with regard to hydrometric schemes, investigation of groundwater resources, minimum acceptable flows, and controlling abstractions of surface and underground water.

(ii) The existing functions in relation to the control of pollution.

(iii) Ensuring that water was made available to meet the needs of water undertakers and (within practical limitations) other abstractors.

(iv) The construction and operation of major conservation schemes.

(v) Co-ordinating its own proposals under (iv) with the proposals of the water undertakers and sewage disposal authorities in its region in order to establish consistent five-year programmes covering all aspects of water functions in the region.

(vi) The existing functions in relation to land drainage.

(vii) The existing functions in relation to fisheries.

(viii) Where applicable, the existing functions in relation to navigation.

(4) The existing committee structure for land drainage, fisheries and pollution control would remain unchanged, but, on account of the reduction in the number of authorities, the work of the committees could cover larger areas and thus the total number of these committees in the country would roughly be halved. Alternatively, the number of committees could remain the same as at present.

218. In other respects, for example the financial arrangements, the considerations which apply to System A (paras. 198-212) would apply equally to System B.

**System C**

219. As we pointed out in para. 126, the evidence we received about the optimum number of river authorities was conflicting. Considerations relating to water supply would suggest a substantial reduction in their number, but, on the other hand, such a reduction might militate against the satisfactory performance of their more local duties connected with land drainage (including sea defence), fisheries and navigation. We have stated in para. 161 that, although we recommend the setting up of RWAs, it is not part of our remit to attempt to determine the most desirable number, a task which would involve many more factors than we can take into account. But if it were eventually decided to have a relatively small number of RWAs, say ten or less, a system of organisation in which all the present functions of river authorities were vested in RWAs would have definite disadvantages.

220. In that case, an alternative intermediate system of organisation which ought to be considered is one in which the number of river authorities remains the same as at the present but the ownership of major water conservation schemes is vested in the RWAs and not in the river authorities. The RWA would also take over the regulatory functions of the present river authorities in relation to abstractions of water and discharges of effluent, and their responsibility for collecting data and carrying out investigations.

221. There would then be 10 or less RWAs in England and Wales with the following functions:

(i) the duties prescribed in the Water Resources Act 1963, with regard to hydrometric schemes, investigation of groundwater resources, minimum acceptable flows, and controlling abstractions of surface and underground water.

(ii) The functions of the present river authorities in relation to the control of pollution.

(iii) Ensuring that water was made available to meet the needs of water undertakers and (within practical limitations) other abstractors.

(iv) The construction and operation of major conservation schemes.

(v) Co-ordinating its own proposals under (iv) with the proposals of the water undertakers and sewage disposal authorities in its region in order to establish consistent five-year programmes covering all aspects of water functions in the region.

The river authorities would retain their responsibilities for land drainage and fisheries and, where applicable, navigation and recreation. And they might also carry out work as agents for the RWA, for example the policing and enforcement of the systems of licences and consents.

222. Broadly speaking the same considerations would apply in System C as in System A (paras. 198-212), except that the RWA would of

course take over responsibility for the charges at present levied on abstractors by river authorities at the same time as it took over their other water conservation functions.

223. We have printed diagrams of Systems B and C in appendix 6, alongside the diagram of System A. The table at the end of this chapter shows the distribution of functions between the different types of authority in Systems A, B and C and compares them with the present system.

## Resolution of conflicts in systems based on single-purpose authorities

224. All the four systems of organisation we have described have in common the existence of RWAs whose duty it is to ensure the formulation of five-year action programmes covering all the separate bodies carrying out water functions in the region. They differ in the character of the RWA, and the choice lies between making the RWA a multi-purpose body dealing with all water functions in the region; making the RWA a single-purpose body dealing only with planning and co-ordination; making the RWA a dual-purpose body combining planning and co-ordination with the water conservation and pollution control functions of the present river authorities; and making the RWA a dual-purpose body combining planning and co-ordination with all the executive functions of the present river authorities. But a very important question is whether a co-ordinated action programme can always be established, and this is a matter which requires clarification. The following seem to be the points of principle involved.

225. Firstly, we are not concerned with the mechanism by which the individual programmes of the operating units in a region are examined, modified if necessary, and consolidated into a self-consistent programme for the whole region. This process depends upon the carrying out of dialogues between the officers of the various bodies concerned, and there are well known techniques of various degrees of complexity for producing and optimising plans for a number of interconnected operations. The function of producing consolidated programmes for consideration by the members is therefore a managerial one.

226. Secondly, the formulation and acceptance of five-year action programmes is not a duty solely of the RWAs. They must be accepted and authorised, in some sense of these words, by the minister. It is not, however, our task to try to lay down what type of information, and in what detail, the minister would require for him to be able to authorise the five-year action programmes of all the statutory bodies concerned with water functions. We are concerned with a different point, namely, what means can be employed to resolve the deadlock which would arise if no agreed programme could be submitted to the minister.

227. This situation can only occur in systems of organisation in which one statutory body has a supervisory role over other statutory bodies, that is, if the system is not based on multi-purpose RWAs. As we have seen in chapter 3, there are substantial difficulties in arriving at agreed solutions in

cases where there are conflicting interests, and there is at present no practical way of resolving them except by the minister, aided by the Water Resources Board, using his powers of persuasion. Admittedly, the minister has important statutory functions which give him considerable influence, for example deciding various kinds of appeals; but these functions are all essentially negative. Under the Water Resources Act 1963 the minister has apparently more far-reaching powers to give directions, and he also has default powers under various Acts which might theoretically be used to resolve deadlocks, but it is not easy to see how these particular powers could be effective in practice. Even if a body could be shown to have defaulted on its duties, and this is most unlikely because most disputes have their origins in differing opinions as to what a body's duties are, it would be extremely difficult to find any other body to take over the duties in question.

228. Are we then no better off with RWAs than without them, in the sense that any of the statutory operating bodies can opt out of the action programme on the grounds that it does not agree with it, and that in practice the only remedy is for the minister and his officials to use their powers of persuasion, a task which they are not organised to do? We do not take such a negative view, for the following reason.

229. The RWA could not be given the duty of producing *agreed* programmes for all the bodies in the region, but it can and would be given the duty of producing self-consistent programmes for these bodies, and if necessary a number of such programmes. If the programme submitted by the RWA to the minister was not an agreed programme, he would enter into appropriate discussions with all concerned, and he would ultimately authorise either the original programme or some modification of it. There could therefore never be a deadlock in the sense that there was no action programme which the minister could authorise, and once a programme had been authorised by the minister we cannot envisage any circumstances in which it would not be carried out to the best of their ability by all concerned. We do not feel called upon to comment on the formal methods which the minister might use to arrive at his decisions.

230. In a system of multi-purpose authorities the conflicts which at present arise because of the existence of separate statutory bodies within the water field would no longer arise in their present form. They would of course not disappear, but they would become internal problems between the various divisions of the RWA, which would have to be resolved by the RWA. In what ways, and to what extent, would a system based on single-purpose authorities resolve the present conflicts? And would the variants of such a system differ in this respect?

231. In so far as reorganisation would increase the average size of water undertakings, it would reduce the problems posed at present by inflexibility in the use of sources and bulk transmission networks (paras. 132-3 and 142-4). Each undertaking would be in a position to redeploy its own sources and transmission networks, if this proved necessary, within an extensive area. However, there would continue to be a considerable number of separate water undertakings in England and Wales (of the order of 50), and so

problems of inflexibility would still arise. These considerations are common to all three variants of a system based on single-purpose authorities.

232. There would always be two, and in one variant three, and perhaps on occasions more, authorities involved in making new sources available for public water supply. Water undertakers would continue to have statutory duties to supply water to consumers; and in Systems B and C the RWA would be responsible for allocating sources to water undertakers and constructing major conservation works to augment supplies. However, it is hoped that the problems at present associated with divided responsibility (paras. 134-9) would be overcome by placing on the RWA a clear statutory duty to make water available to water undertakers. Under System A the situation would be somewhat more complex than at present: the water undertaker would rely on the RWA to find a way of meeting his increased demand for water as part of its planning functions, but the responsibility for constructing, owning and operating any major conservation schemes that were necessary would lie with a third body, the river authority.

233. Unless the number of river authorities were reduced at the same time as RWAs were established, the responsibility for the construction, ownership and operation of major water conservation schemes under System A would lie with the same number of bodies as at present, and the areas over which the costs of such schemes would be spread would be the same as at present. Without such a reduction, therefore, the difficulties associated with joint schemes (paras. 140-1) would remain, except to the extent that the number of such schemes was reduced by the reduction in the number of water undertakers. In Systems B and C, however, the number of authorities responsible for major water conservation schemes would be substantially reduced, and the areas over which the costs of such schemes would be spread would be significantly extended. The number of joint schemes necessary would thereby be reduced. The benefit would be greater under System C than under System B because the number of RWAs envisaged is smaller. In both systems some joint schemes would continue to be necessary between individual RWAs and probably also between RWAs and water undertakers. However, as in a system of multi-purpose authorities (para. 188), an important factor is the role which would be assumed by the national water authority, a question we discuss in chapter 6.

234. The basic conflict of interest between abstractors and dischargers in relation to the treatment required to produce effluents of higher than Royal Commission standard would be mitigated by the availability of grants from the river authority or the RWA, as the case may be (para. 210). Both this conflict and the much more difficult conflict over the treatment required to bring effluents on heavily polluted rivers up to Royal Commission standard would be mitigated by the drastic reduction in the number of authorities responsible for sewage disposal, which would spread the costs involved over more extensive areas. A further reduction in conflicts might in theory be secured by the establishment of equalisation schemes to even out the incidence of costs between separate statutory bodies, but, for the reasons given there, we have rejected the idea of going beyond what is suggested in paras. 209-10. All these considerations apply equally to all three variants of a system based on single-purpose authorities.

235. In so far as the conflicts of interest we identified in chapter 3 were not removed or mitigated in a system of organisation based on single-purpose authorities, and in so far as they could not be resolved at the local level, the main mechanism for resolving them would be the process consisting of the formulation of action programmes, their submission to the minister and their acceptance by the minister, as we have described it in paras. 225-9. In particular, this would be the means of resolving conflicts over proposals by the RWA which entailed positive action on the part of another body.

236. However, the minister would continue to have available other means of resolving conflicts between separate statutory bodies. Thus he would decide appeals by water undertakers against decisions by river authorities or RWAs, as the case may be, in relation to abstraction licences. He would also decide references by sewage disposal authorities over decisions by river authorities or RWAs, as the case may be, in relation to consents to discharge.

**Conclusions**

237. To sum up, all three of the systems of organisation based on single-purpose authorities which we have described (Systems A, B and C) would reduce the conflicts of interest that exist at present. We have already mentioned above some of the considerations which would lead to a preference for one of these systems over the others. In the light of the foregoing discussion we can now set out the arguments for and against each variant in more detail.

*System A*

238. System A is the one in which RWAs are placed over river authorities, as planning and co-ordinating bodies without executive functions. This variant asserts unambiguously that planning and co-ordination is a separate function. The areas and constitutions of river authorities might remain as at present, if that were thought desirable, while at the same time the areas and constitutions of the RWAs could be closely related to their own particular function. If there were no reduction in the number of river authorities, there would be less disruption than there would be in establishing System B or C. River authorities would lose their present responsibility for planning but, in spite of its intrinsic importance, this is of only minor significance in terms of expenditure and numbers of staff. The substantial reduction in the number of bodies responsible for water supply and sewage disposal is of course common to all the variants.

239. On the other hand, unless the number of river authorities was substantially reduced, some of them would not be strong enough to handle successfully the construction, ownership and operation of major conservation schemes. Moreover, because their areas would still be relatively small, the number of joint schemes would not be greatly reduced, and in this respect the present conflicts of interest would persist. Indeed, a total of 29 river authorities would be not much less numerous than the 50 or so water undertakers which would exist after reorganisation, and in terms of annual expenditure or professional staff they would often be substantially smaller.

If we assume that the number of river authorities would in fact be substantially reduced, System A loses its attractiveness in terms of the relative lack of disruption. Whatever the number of river authorities, there would in System A be three types of body involved in obtaining supplies of water for the water undertaker in place of the present two; but, in contrast to the present situation, the roles of the different types of body would be clearly defined. The river authority would no longer be the sole judge as to what actions are required of it.

### System B

240. System B is the one in which the number of river authorities is reduced by about half and they become the RWAs. This system emphasises the connection between the existing regulatory and planning functions of river authorities and the more far-reaching planning and co-ordination which we believe to be necessary in future. There would certainly be stronger bodies at the regional level to handle major conservation schemes than exist at present. But two questions remain to be answered. Would the number of joint schemes and the conflicts of interest associated with them be sufficiently reduced? And would this number of RWAs fulfil our criteria for the regions within which planning and co-ordination ought to be carried out?

241. If the answer to either of these questions is negative, then System B would have definite disadvantages. Some of the functions which RWAs would take over from river authorities, for example land drainage, have a strong local element, and there are limits on the size of area over which they can be successfully administered. If the needs of water conservation and planning and co-ordination turn out to require fewer than about fifteen bodies, then they may conflict with the needs of other functions such as land drainage, and such a conflict could not be easily resolved within a single body of the type envisaged. For example, if the number of RWAs was reduced much below fifteen it might be difficult, because of the size of the areas involved and the number of local authorities they would contain, to retain a constitution modelled on that of the present river authorities. If weight was attached to the considerations stated in paras. 206-7, they would lead to the conclusion that this particular constitution would in any case be inappropriate for an RWA.

### System C

242. System C is the one in which RWAs are established in addition to river authorities, but take over from them not only their present planning functions but also certain of their executive functions. It is envisaged that the RWAs would be relatively few in number, probably not more than ten and perhaps as few as six. If it were to be concluded that both planning and co-ordination and the executive responsibility for water conservation required significantly fewer than about fifteen bodies, then System C would have a definite advantage. It would also have an advantage if the view were taken that, disregarding these functions, the present number of river authorities is roughly right for their remaining functions and ought not to be

reduced. Moreover, whatever view is taken as to the maximum number of bodies that ought to be entrusted with planning and co-ordination and the executive responsibility for water conservation, System C goes further than System A or B in reducing the number of joint schemes and the problems associated with them, including inflexibility.

243. There are, however, arguments against System C. It can be argued that the present executive functions of river authorities constitute a single task of river management, and that distributing these functions between separate statutory bodies would lead to a loss of efficiency. If this argument is accepted it follows that System C would create new problems of divided responsibility which do not exist at present. If river authorities were to act as executive agents for RWAs in regard to certain functions, as was envisaged in para. 221, it might be unclear in practice where responsibility lay even within sub-divisions of river management such as pollution control. Moreover, because river authorities would have fewer functions than at present, there could be doubt about their ability to attract and retain able members and expert staff.

244. We have now described the alternative systems of organisation that might be established to achieve the degree of planning and co-ordination we believe to be necessary: on the one hand the systems based on single-purpose authorities which we have just discussed, on the other hand the system of multi-purpose authorities we described at the beginning of this chapter. In chapter 8 we give our general conclusions about their respective merits. Before doing so, however, we look at two important questions we have not so far examined: the role of the national water authority in relation to the construction, ownership and operation of major conservation schemes; and the position of Wales.

TABLE    SYSTEMS BASED ON SINGLE-PURPOSE AUTHORITIES

DISTRIBUTION OF FUNCTIONS BETWEEN DIFFERENT TYPES OF AUTHORITY

| | Present system | SYSTEM A RWAs without operational responsibilities | SYSTEM B RWAs and river authorities combined | SYSTEM C RWAs with some operational responsibilities |
|---|---|---|---|---|
| NUMBER OF RWAs | — | 6 to 15 | about 15 | 6 to 10 |
| **FUNCTION** | | | | |
| **OVERALL PLANNING AND CO-ORDINATION** | | | | |
| Preparing and securing the implementation of the national plan | Water Resources Board in conjunction with minister | national authority | national authority | national authority |
| Preparing and securing the implementation of regional plans and action programmes incorporating elements of the national plan | (river authorities prepare plan for their area) | RWAs | RWAs | RWAs |
| Responsibility for ensuring that water undertakers and other direct abstractors have sufficient water | (imprecisely defined, see paras. 134-9) | RWAs | RWAs | RWAs |
| Control of abstractions through the licensing system (including policing and enforcement) | river authorities | river authorities | RWAs | RWAs but using river authorities as their agents |
| Management of water quality (including the consent procedure for discharges, policing and enforcement) | river authorities | river authorities | RWAs | RWAs but using river authorities as their agents |

67

## RIVER MANAGEMENT

| | Present system | A | B | C |
|---|---|---|---|---|
| Hydrometric work and investigations of underground strata | river authorities under supervision of WRB | river authorities under supervision of national authority | RWAs under supervision of national authority | RWAs under supervision of national authority and using river authorities as their agents |
| Construction, ownership and operation of major conservation schemes, including river regulation schemes, multi-purpose schemes and strategic transmission aqueducts | river authorities alone or in combination with water undertakers | as at present | RWAs alone or in combination with water undertakers | RWAs alone or in combination with water undertakers |
| Construction, ownership and operation of river works for water quality improvement | river authorities | river authorities | RWAs | RWAs |
| Land drainage and sea defence | river authorities | river authorities | RWAs | river authorities |
| Fisheries | river authorities | river authorities | RWAs | river authorities |
| Navigation and recreation | river authorities, British Waterways Board and other bodies | as at present | RWAs, British Waterways Board and other bodies | as at present |

## WATER SUPPLY

| | Present system | A | B | C |
|---|---|---|---|---|
| Responsibility for meeting the demands of consumers for water | water undertakings owned by local authorities, joint boards or companies | as at present | as at present | as at present |
| Construction, ownership and operation of sources, intakes and trunk mains other than those included above under RIVER MANAGEMENT | water undertakings owned by local authorities, joint boards or companies (and other licensed abstractors) | as at present | as at present | as at present |
| Treatment and distribution | water undertakings owned by local authorities, joint boards or companies (and other licensed abstractors) | as at present | as at present | as at present |

## SEWERAGE AND SEWAGE DISPOSAL

| | Present system | A | B | C |
|---|---|---|---|---|
| Ownership and operation of public on-site sewers | local authorities | local authorities | local authorities | local authorities |
| Construction, ownership and operation of off-site and trunk sewers | local authorities or joint boards | sewage disposal units owned by local authorities or joint boards | sewage disposal units owned by local authorities or joint boards | sewage disposal units owned by local authorities or joint boards |
| Construction, ownership and operation of sewage disposal works and other water reclamation works | local authorities or joint boards (and private dischargers) | sewage disposal units owned by local authorities or joint boards (and private dischargers) | sewage disposal units owned by local authorities or joint boards (and private dischargers) | sewage disposal units owned by local authorities or joint boards (and private dischargers) |
| Control over the reception of trade effluents to all sewers | local authorities or joint boards | sewage disposal units owned by local authorities or joint boards | sewage disposal units owned by local authorities or joint boards | sewage disposal units owned by local authorities or joint boards |

## 6. THE ROLE OF THE NATIONAL WATER AUTHORITY

245. In chapter 4 we described the combination of plans we consider to be necessary for the effective planning and co-ordination of water use: the national plan, the regional plan, and the transformation of these into five-year action programmes at the regional level. We envisaged that the production of the national long-term plan would be the responsibility of a national water authority. We now look at the question of what other functions this authority should perform.

246. We assume that the future national authority would in any case be responsible for the functions at present performed by the Water Resources Board. That is to say, in addition to formulating the national plan, it would give technical guidance to the bodies at the regional level, it would collate and publish hydrometric data, and it would carry out and supervise research. In addition, we believe that it should carry out these functions over a much wider field than the present Board, in that it should deal not merely with water conservation in the sense of the 1963 Act but with all the relevant aspects of water management, and in particular water quality (para. 152).

247. We do not exclude the possibility that within this wider field the authority would also perform other functions of a supervisory or specialist character appropriate to a central body. As we said at the beginning of our report, we were not asked to look at the more specialised aspects of water services. But clearly the national authority would have a much more extensive interest in research than the present Board, an interest which would spring from a close concern with the practical applications of research. It would therefore be in a good position to foster interdisciplinary studies of water problems. A central body would also have a very considerable interest in training, and indeed other matters. The role which it was appropriate for it to play in each of these matters would have to be the subject of detailed study in each case in the light of the functions of other existing bodies.

248. Our primary concern, however, is with planning and co-ordination and with the implementation of plans. Like the Water Resources Board, the national authority would have a continuing responsibility for monitoring the implementation of the national plan which it had formulated. But should it do more than this? We have already described systems of organisation whose constituent bodies would, we believe, be capable of carrying out the great majority of projects in the regional action programmes. However, there will be a certain category of projects included in the national plan, major water storage projects and distribution networks of the kind now emerging from the Water Resources Board's studies, which will serve very wide areas. We have in mind particularly some of the projects put forward in the Board's report on the North, and the central distribution network now under consideration for South East England.[1] The question of the location of responsibility for implementing projects of this kind requires further examination.

249. Among the suggestions put to us were the following three: that the Water Resources Board should be given powers to construct, own and operate major projects itself, and if necessary acquire existing works; that

1 These are described in Appendix D to the Board's Seventh Annual Report.

there should be a second national authority responsible for major projects, existing side by side with the authority responsible for national planning; and that *ad hoc* authorities should be set up for individual projects, analogous to the present joint water authorities and bulk supply boards.

250. It can be argued that there would be advantages in combining the responsibility for planning and implementation within a single statutory body. On the other hand, it is also arguable that there is an important role for a national water authority as advisers to ministers and their departments, and that this role is incompatible with any direct executive responsibilities. Again, the establishment of *ad hoc* bodies might lead to an undesirable degree of fragmentation and rigidity. We did not feel able to enter deeply into the merits of the various alternatives, particularly as we were not asked to examine the form of organisation at the national level; and in any case the choice between them resolves itself to a large extent into a question of practical management. For the same reasons we did not try to discuss the constitution of the future body or bodies at national level, and whether it should differ from that of the present Water Resources Board.

251. From the point of view of our particular task, the central question is whether any of the devices suggested in para. 249 is necessary, or whether all likely water conservation projects could be successfully carried out by the bodies we have already postulated at regional and local levels, either alone or in combination.

252. The answer does not depend merely on whether projects will be undertaken to serve several regions. Given the existence of strong bodies at the regional level, and given adequate powers on the part of the national water authority and/or the minister, it will be quite possible in simple cases to ensure that such a project is carried out by the regional bodies concerned. More complex projects might also be carried out in this way. As we noted above, discussions are taking place between the five river authorities involved about the implementation of a regional distribution network for the central area of South East England, as envisaged in the Water Resources Board's studies. But there are certain inherent disadvantages attached to joint schemes, and with progressively more complex projects there will come a point where there is a clear balance of advantage from the point of view of efficiency in a scheme being carried out by a single body.

253. Whether that point will be reached in practice in England and Wales in the remainder of this century cannot be determined with certainty at the present moment. The answer might in fact depend on which of the alternative strategies explored in the Water Resources Board's studies are actually chosen. But if a particular strategy can be shown to be the best on all other grounds, it should not have to be rejected because of any doubts about the ability of the system of organisation to carry it out successfully.

254. We conclude that in order to meet this situation there ought in future to be a national authority with reserve powers to acquire, construct, own and operate works itself, powers which would have to be activated by an order made by the relevant minister. We believe powers of this kind would escape the objection normally urged against a default power, that the body

possessing the default power is incapable of carrying out the relevant function itself because it lacks the necessary staff etc. It would be for the minister to decide in advance, in the light of all the circumstances and any representations made to him by the national authority or by other bodies, whether any forthcoming project ought to be carried out by the national authority. If he decided that it should, the authority might either set up an operational division, which would then be available to handle further projects, or engage appropriate consultants. The reason for giving the authority a reserve power of this kind from the beginning is that it would be in a position to undertake a project when the need arose, without waiting for further legislation.

255. While we believe that the solution just suggested will provide a satisfactory answer to the problem of implementing the largest projects, we recognise that in taking on executive responsibilities of this kind the national authority would inevitably change its nature to some extent. As we have said, such a change might be thought prejudicial to the authority's role as advisers to the minister and to the bodies at the regional level. If the minister took this view he could still proceed by setting up a new *ad hoc* authority for that particular project.

256. We do not exclude the possibility that after the national authority had been empowered to carry out a given project, it might decide to do so in collaboration with some or all of the river authorities or RWAs concerned (according to which of the systems of organisation described in chapter 5 is adopted), or use them as its agents for the construction or operation. But the national authority would carry the ultimate responsibility for the project and obtain all the necessary authorisations. Its expenditure on individual projects would be recovered from the relevant river authorities or RWAs.

257. The considerations advanced above apply in principle whichever of the alternative systems of organisation is adopted. However, the actual position will vary according to the number of bodies that are made responsible for water conservation at the regional level. The larger the number of such bodies, the greater the chance that the point described in para. 252 will be reached, where either the responsibility for a particular project has to be taken out of their hands or a stategy has to be rejected because of doubts about the possibility of implementing it.

258. When in chapter 8 we attempt to assess the merits of the systems of organisation described in chapter 5, we shall do so on the assumption that there will be a body at the national level with reserve powers to acquire, construct, own and operate works itself.

## 7. THE POSITION OF WALES

259. Although, under the terms of the relevant transfer of functions Orders, appointments to the Central Advisory Water Committee are the responsibility of the Secretary of State for the Environment, we are also required to give advice to the Secretary of State for Wales. The reappointment of the Committee on the present occasion was made in consultation with the

then Secretary of State. And we have had the needs of Wales in mind, equally with those of England, in our deliberations. All the conclusions and recommendations elsewhere in our report are of general application. But there are certain further points which we think it necessary to make in relation to Wales.

260. The Welsh Council provided us with copies of a report by their Water Committee on 'Water in Wales' which they submitted to the Secretary of State for Wales in June 1970. Members of the Council gave oral evidence to us, and subsequently sent us a supplementary note on some of the points we had raised. In view of the fact that we had been asked to examine future organisation, the Council's report dealt with this aspect of the matter only in general terms. But they expressed the hope that their report would enable us to appreciate their concern that development of the water resources of Wales should, in the words of the White Paper 'Wales the Way Ahead", be 'used and controlled to the widest public benefit and with the fullest safeguards for Welsh interests'.

261. The Council concluded that heavy reliance on upland reservoirs would remain even after the development of other types of source. They accepted the validity of the concept of unified management of a river basin, based on natural boundaries rather than political and administrative boundaries. However, they considered that the present constitution of river authorities (which is determined insofar as the local authority members are concerned by rateable value) does not give sufficient representation to areas affected by proposals to build reservoirs. They drew attention to the sense of injustice caused by the present arrangements for compensation for land acquired for reservoirs. And they recommended that consideration should be given to the establishment of appropriate financial and administrative arrangements which would arise from the adoption of the principle that continuing income should be received by rural areas in which reservoirs are located in addition to the revenue they receive in the form of rate income. All these issues are common to England and to Wales.

262. The Council suggest as a method by which Welsh rural areas might receive a continuing income the setting up of a Water Development Authority for Wales. They envisage that this authority would be responsible for building new reservoirs in Wales, and might also take over any existing reservoir whose function had changed. To this extent, it would operate in accordance with strategies and requirements formulated by other bodies. However, it would be given powers to develop the maximum potentialities of water resources by, for example, being itself responsible for recreational and tourist uses, and it would be required to have regard to the interests of the communities in the areas in which reservoirs are built. The Council consider that the existence of such an authority would reduce the significance of the difficulty over the constitution of river authorities referred to above, and that, because they see the authority mainly as an agency of a commercial character, it would be easier to deal in this context with the question of compensation.

263. We have set out our own views on the subject of compensation in

1  Cmnd. 3334.

74

the note on difficulties over the building of new reservoirs which appears as appendix 3 to this report. We are in general agreement with the Council in wanting to see the recreational potential of reservoirs, a subject which they investigated in some detail, developed as fully as possible. We note with satisfaction their findings that properly developed recreational facilities can be an economic proposition, and that in addition to direct benefits considerable indirect benefits can accrue to nearby small towns and the surrounding rural area.

264. Financial arrangements are outside our own terms of reference. We have not therefore examined the justification for the payment of a subsidy (over and above adequate compensation and the payment of rates) to areas in which reservoirs are located.[1] Even if the case for such a subsidy could be made out, it would not in itself entail the establishment of a separate statutory body. We have noted the argument which has been put forward that the creation of a Welsh Water Development Authority would have psychological advantages in encouraging a more favourable attitude towards reservoirs in Wales. We are in full agreement with any action which would reduce opposition to the building of reservoirs, but we foresee insuperable difficulties in any of the systems of organisation we have examined in involving another statutory body directly in the construction and operation of reservoirs, as distinct, say, from exploiting their recreational and tourist potential.

265. As long as the Secretary of State for Wales retains the ultimate power to approve or reject proposals for water conservation schemes in Wales, then Welsh interests are safeguarded.

266. It would appear to us, however, that a body similar to the present Welsh Committee of the Water Resources Board (para. 91) could play a useful part in the consideration of problems of water use and river management in Wales, and could advise the future national authority on such matters of this kind as may be referred to it by the Secretary of State for Wales. After the reorganisation of the administrative system for the control of the water cycle has taken place, a committee might be established on these lines which would include representatives from the national authority and the Welsh and Anglo-Welsh Regional Water Authorities and, if a system of organisation based on single-purpose authorities were to be adopted, from the other types of body concerned with water in Wales.

267. We now go back to the alternative system of organisation we described in chapter 5 and state, in the following chapter, our conclusions about their respective merits.

## 8. THE AREA FOR DECISION

### INTRODUCTION

268. Once we had identified the new procedures that are required to deal with the problems described in chapter 3, and had clarified our ideas about

---

1 As we noted in para. 57, water conservation works owned by river authorities would not be liable to rates as the law stands at present. However, we understand that the government accepts in principle that they should be liable to rates and will introduce amending legislation as soon as possible.

the possible types of organisation needed to carry out these procedures, it might have been expected that the remaining task of deciding which organisation was the best one would be relatively simple. But this was not so, and, in spite of prolonged discussions, no unanimous view has emerged. The principal reason for this is as follows.

269. In trying to compare the merits of the systems of organisation described in chapter 5, it is necessary to bear in mind that many of the improvements envisaged would be made with equal ease or equal difficulty whichever system was adopted. Others would be more difficult to make in one system than in another, but all of them could in principle be made in any of the systems. It is therefore difficult to see how there can be any objective method of assessing the relative merits of the various systems, and one is reduced to making subjective judgments concerning how much more difficult it would be to formulate plans and take actions in one type of organisation as compared with another.

270. In making such subjective judgments, it is, of course, helpful if one can analyse the advantages and disadvantages of various courses of action in the light of generally accepted principles or criteria. There are in fact a number of principles which might be so used, but none of these would receive unqualified acceptance by all members of the Committee. For example, some members feel that every effort should be made to preserve the existing links between water functions and local authorities. Others feel that a loosening of some of these links is inevitable and indeed desirable, while a substantial number of members feel that it is difficult to take such arguments into account when the future pattern of local government is unknown and the success of its future working is unpredictable. Some members would go even further and would maintain that political considerations such as these should not be taken into account by the Committee: it is for ministers to do so. However, even if the Committee had agreed that political or semi-political considerations should be explicitly excluded, it is impossible to ensure that they are not implicit factors in members' judgments, and in any event our terms of reference ask us to consider our problems in the light of the Report of the Royal Commission on Local Government in England.

271. Another line or argument which might seem helpful is that, since water functions are becoming more and more interlinked and therefore multi-purpose, they should be dealt with by multi-purpose bodies. But a counter-argument is that multi-purpose functions, unless they are of a very simple nature, involve several distinct types of activities, and the organisation can only be run efficiently if it is divided into a number of specialist sections. Whether these sections should be divisions or whether they should have separate corporate identities depends on how closely interlinked the functions are, and this cannot be settled by an appeal to general principles.

272. Since the Committee was unable, without very substantial individual reservations, to come to a decision about the superiority of any of the systems of organisation we have put forward, we felt that it would not be helpful to try to summarise the arguments for and against them. The characteristics of each system are fully described in chapter 5, and it is

clear from the descriptions given there what the merits of each system are. A summary of the merits of one system in comparison with another would merely consist of a condensed paraphrase of those features which are present in the first and lacking in the second, while the demerits of the first system would be those features present in the second and lacking in the first. For similar reasons we felt that it would not be helpful to try to evaluate the merits of the various systems in the light of such tenets as 'water services are an integral part of local government functions' or 'multi-purpose services ought to be carried out by multi-purpose bodies'. These tenets are conclusions and not starting points, and no arguments are needed to show that single-purpose organisations are consistent with the first tenet and that multi-purpose organisations are consistent with the second: they have been constructed to be so. We therefore felt that it would be most useful to ministers if we were to set out those factors which must be taken into account in coming to a decision, which are specific to our remit and which are not immediately obvious.

## THE POSITION OF LAND DRAINAGE AND FISHERIES

273. Two of the major functions of the existing river authorities, land drainage and fisheries, are not within our present terms of reference except to the extent that they might be affected by any proposed changes, because there are no problems of organisation in these fields comparable to those relating to water conservation and the control of pollution. Nevertheless we have had to have regard in our work to the whole field of water administration, and there are certain points we want to make about these particular services. If the size of local administrative units were substantially increased, if there were changes in the balance of functions and if agricultural interests (which are an integral part of most land drainage schemes) are to continue to be taken fully into account, then the impact of all these factors on land drainage must be given due weight. In short it will be necessary to bear in mind the effect of changes to the present structure of water administration on the land drainage function of river authorities.

274. As for fisheries, because they are affected by every aspect of water management, use and development, their interests too cannot be excluded from consideration in reorganisation. The Jeger Report, and subsequently the River Survey conducted by the National Federation of Anglers, have shown that water pollution and other problems of concern to anglers are so widespread that they cannot be resolved at the local level. In order to ensure that continuity in the conservation and control of fisheries is maintained, there should be close collaboration at river basin level between fisheries and all other water functions and interests; and there should be representation of fisheries interests at all levels where water planning takes place. The Water Resources Board very soon recognised this problem and maintain regular meetings at chairman, member and chief officer level with members of the Salmon and Trout Association and the National Federation of Anglers; in addition, to assist their understanding of the relationship between fisheries, river management and the research needs, they have formed an informal advisory committee of recognised experts on fishery research and management. We are told these committees have been most

useful, and they should clearly be retained in some form, whether on a statutory basis or, as now, on a voluntary basis.

## THE MAIN ARGUMENTS

275. If our task had been to set up an organisation to carry out certain functions which were entirely new, it would have been easier, but this is not so. We are not concerned with new functions but with old ones which are changing in magnitude and complexity. This means that we have to take into account the principle, which we all accept, that an existing organisation should not be changed for another one unless it can clearly be demonstrated that the new organisation is superior. But the application of this principle is not as simple as it may seem at first sight. It is clear that a multi-purpose type of organisation is far removed from what exists at the moment. However, all the single-purpose systems of organisation proposed also differ from the present system. They are similar to it in that the constituent bodies are enlarged versions of the existing ones, but the relationship between the various bodies would be very substantially altered. The alteration would be least in the system where all the functions of river authorities are transferred to Regional Water Authorities. Thus the case for multi-purpose authorities needs to be substantially stronger than that for single-purpose authorities, and those of us who come down in favour of multi-purpose authorities do so, not necessarily because they feel that multi-purpose authorities are better than single-purpose authorities, but because they believe that the problems of the next thirty years are such that they cannot be dealt with by single-purpose authorities. Those of us who are in favour of single-purpose authorities believe, on the other hand, that one or other of the variants described in chapter 5 will prove to be best.

276. The real question at issue is the division of duties between central and local government, and the future of water services is part of this much larger question, on which anything we might say would be superfluous. On the narrower issue some of us would say that the present constitutional structure, in which the major part of water services is controlled by local government and the remainder by statutory companies, ought to continue. These members feel that, on the one hand, this would give the best prospect of overcoming one of the major obstacles to progress, namely the problem of meeting the wishes of local people, and, on the other, would be consistent with the general wish to see local government strengthened.

277. Those members feel serious doubts about the capacity of a multi-purpose authority, covering a very wide area, to cultivate that intimate and confidential relationship with local government so necessary to handle successfully the explosive reactions of public opinion to most major projects concerning rivers and water.

278. Other members take the view that there are no overwhelming reasons for the continuance of the present constitutional structure, other than that relating to land drainage, fisheries, and navigation and recreation. In their view the vital question is not whether the present constitutional structure should or should not remain unchanged, but whether it can remain so.

279. We all agree that water services are becoming increasingly multi-purpose ones and that the various activities must be co-ordinated throughout fairly extensive regions. We also all agree that this co-ordination must be carried out by Regional Water Authorities which will have extensive new powers and responsibilities. Whichever system of organisation is chosen, success will depend upon these authorities being sufficiently strong. But this could lead to a situation in which the autonomy of the operating bodies was so limited that they could not be considered as being independent statutory bodies, and in that case a single-purpose system would become untenable. The question what degree of independence a body must possess in order for it to be a statutory body is not capable of a precise answer, and it is therefore not surpising that we have divided views on this extremely important matter.

280. We believe that, with any of the systems of organisation described in chapter 5, it will be possible, provided that the Regional Water Authority is strong enough (and this is a very important proviso), to arrive at action programmes which are the most efficient on technical grounds and the most economic in financial terms, and which would best subserve the development plans of local authorities. Whether these action programmes are acceptable to the general public, and, if they are not, what modifications would make them so, can only be determined by a variety of consultations, some of which would culminate in public inquiries. Some of us believe that the differences between the various systems of organisation would not be a major factor in the general course of events leading up to a public inquiry, or in the evidence presented there or in the final outcome. Others hold the views set out in paras. 276-7.

281. One of the most important stumbling-blocks to progress is not what should be done, but at whose expense it should be carried out. Finance is at the root of many of the conflicts of interest described in chapter 3. All the members of the Committee are convinced that the number of statutory bodies in the water field must be drastically reduced. But, if the number of statutory bodies is to be of the order of 100 to 200, the increasing transfers of water from one river basin to another and the growth in the reuse of water will mean that within the next ten years or so a substantial proportion of the costs which are attributable to new works will relate to services provided by one body for another body. In other words, after the costs incurred by a body on new works for its own benefit have been calculated, there will, in many cases, be an element of common costs to be recovered by the allocation of charges to a number of bodies. It is then necessary to find some equitable method of spreading these common costs, and the most certain way of achieving this is to form the various bodies into larger groups and to equalise the charges accordingly.

282. In so far as the costs to be equalised are those which are internal to a region, this can be done by aggregating the relevant costs of all the bodies in that region. But if the total costs of all the bodies were aggregated in this way, the bodies would have no independent existence, which is a characteristic of what we mean by a multi-purpose authority. As time goes on, the cost of new works is bound to become a more and more important

financial factor, and the advantages of a multi-purpose system of organisation will therefore increase.

283. Some of us believe the arguments for a multi-purpose system of organisation to be decisive, and therefore have come down in favour of it. As regards the number of Regional Water Authorities, one of the most important criteria, which applies to all the systems of organisation, is as follows. Each region would have to be sufficiently large, and its income sufficiently great, for the inter-regional costs arising from inter-regional water transfers to be a relatively small proportion of the total costs, since otherwise the result would be intractable problems concerning the allocation of the inter-regional costs. Even if the relevant information were available, which it is not, it would not have been possible for us to investigate how few regions there might have to be to meet this criterion. But we believe that the number would be small.

284. Those of us who have come down in favour of a multi-purpose organisation have gone on to consider how best to incorporate into this system all the features that we all consider desirable, such as adequate public accountability and satisfactory arrangements for the restoration and preservation of our rivers as amenities. These members consider that the multipurpose organisation described in chapter 5 meets these requirements.

285. Other members of the Committee believe that the financial problems will not prove to be so intractable as is argued in the preceding paragraphs. As stated in para. 209 it is possible to equalise certain costs in a singlepurpose system of organisation, though we have found no means of equalising others which would not involve too large an erosion of the financial responsibilities of the constituent bodies. However, this does not mean that it will be impossible to find an equitable basis for common action between the statutory bodies which must exist within a region if a system of singlepurpose authorities is to be viable. Those of us who favour single-purpose authorities believe that it will be possible to solve the financial problems not covered by equalisation schemes through negotiations between the separate statutory bodies.

286. In arriving at our conclusions we have each of us had to take a largely subjective view of the magnitude of the financial problems which would need to be resolved if there were a large number of statutory bodies. These problems are with us to a certain extent at the moment and are increasing, but whether they will become acute or not will probably not be known for some ten years. We are, however, all agreed that they will be difficult.

287. We have so far, in this chapter, referred to systems of single-purpose authorities in general without differentiating between the variants described in chapter 5. The merits and demerits of each of these are implicit in their descriptions, and the variants seek, each in its own way, to ensure, among other objectives, that the Regional Water Authorities are as strong as possible. The thorough-going single-purpose system (System A) seeks to achieve this by devolving as many of the executive functions as possible to the operating bodies, thereby enabling the Regional Water Authorities to concentrate on their primary task of planning and co-ordination. The

system in which all the functions of river authorities are transferred to Regional Water Authorities (System B) seeks to make the Regional Water Authorities as strong as possible by building on the existing foundations, while the system in which the Regional Water Authorities are responsible for all major conservation works as well as for planning and co-ordination (System C) is based upon the principle of dividing the existing functions of river authorities into those which are truly local in character (broadly speaking, the functions which were carried out by river boards), and those which can only be planned and executed on a regional basis.

288. The difficulty in assessing the merits of the different variants of the single-purpose system means that it would be desirable to have a system which was sufficiently flexible for it to be possible to change readily from one variant to another if circumstances justified it. This, however, is not possible in the context of statutory authorities, which must have their duties closely defined by legislation. The choice would therefore have to be made by ministers in the light of the facts known to them at the time of decision, and, once made, it could not be changed except by further legislation.

289. A major factor in assessing the relative merits of systems A, B and C is the view taken about how difficult it would be to deal with the future financial problems in a single-purpose system. If the difficulties were to be severe, as some of us fear that they would be, they could only be reduced to manageable proportions if the number of Regional Water Authorities was small and the degree of equalisation of costs large. Some of us think that the only single-purpose organisation that could be viable in these circumstances would be System C, in which the present duties of river authorities are split, and the ownership of all major water conservation works is vested in the Regional Water Authorities.

290. Those of us who come down in favour of multi-purpose authorities still think that, even with as few as seven regional authorities, and whatever the future structure of local government might be, the single-purpose system would run into great financial problems in implementing plans to develop water resources and to clean up the rivers in the polluted industrial areas. This, in their opinion, could only be done by such extensive directions by the regional authorities through the minister as to make it very dubious whether the water supply and sewage disposal authorities had sufficient autonomy to be considered as statutory bodies and not as agents of central government.

291. One further factor on which we have divided views is whether there would be a major difference between the transitional problems which will arise in setting up the various types of organisation. Some of us feel that the easiest change is to the single-purpose organisation which builds directly on the existing structure by adding to river authorities' existing powers and halving their number. Those of us who favour this solution see the avoidance of the dislocation of a radical change in structure, and the maintaining of the impetus of the present river authorities' programme of water conservation, as decisive for the current decade and therefore of significant importance in the scope of our total remit.

292. Others of us disagree with this argument, because they believe that none of the organisations we have considered can be set up without considerable delay and dislocation. It will take time for legislation to be introduced and passed, and, until this is done, there are very few preliminary steps, if any, which can be taken in anticipation of the reallocation of existing functions, the assumption of new functions and the redeployment of skilled manpower. These members therefore feel that this is a factor which should not be taken into account unless the other arguments are so finely balanced as to make a choice on them alone impossible. The aim must be to determine what form of organisation is best suited to deal with the problems up to the end of this century. Only when this has been settled will it be possible to see what actions can be taken to minimise the inevitable transitional problems.

293. It will not be known with certainty for some considerable time how severe some of the problems will turn out to be, and it is obviously attractive to try to make only those changes now which are bound to be needed in any event, leaving it open for more radical changes to be made later. Some of us feel that this would be a wise course to follow if the later changes could be effected without the need for legislation to alter the constitution and powers of the various bodies concerned. But because of the inflexible nature of statutory bodies it is most unlikely that it would be possible for the transition from one type of organisation to another to be made by a series of gradual changes. These members therefore feel that it would be most undesirable to adopt any form of organisation which, though adequate to deal with present problems, would clearly require, in the foreseeable future, substantial modifications involving new legislation. But other members consider that the need for increased water supplies is already so acute in some parts of the country that the structural changes to be made must cater adequately for the short-term problems, as well as paving the way to provide the right solution to the organisational problems up to the end of the century. These members therefore consider that comparatively simple legislation now is essential, and that further legislation before the end of the century would not be inappropriate.

294. In conclusion we wish to stress once more the necessity to press on as rapidly as possible with the provision of increased supplies of water. This can only be done by the determination of everyone concerned to avoid any further unnecessary delays in implementing proposals currently under study.

## 9. SUMMARY OF CONCLUSIONS AND RECOMMENDATIONS

295. A significant part of our report is taken up with describing the bodies mentioned in our terms of reference as they exist at present. Another large part of the report is devoted to setting out in some detail the alternative systems of organisation that might be established for the future.

296. There are four basic functions which must be carried out: water supply, sewage disposal, river management, and planning and co-ordination. We envisage that in future the last function will be the responsibility partly of the Water Resources Board, enlarged to become a national water authority, and partly of some six to fifteen Regional Water Authorities.

297. One way of organising the four basic functions would be to make the Regional Water Authorities multi-purpose bodies directly responsible for all four functions. In principle a body of this type would raise its revenue by making economic charges for its services. Various safeguards would be retained or introduced to ensure public accountability.

298. The alternative to a system of multi-purpose authorities is a system based on single-purpose authorities, which might mean either

(A) confining the Regional Water Authorities to planning and co-ordination, and retaining river authorities, water undertakers and sewage disposal authorities;

(B) making the river authorities into Regional Water Authorities, and retaining water undertakers and sewage disposal authorities;

(C) retaining river authorities, water undertakers and sewage disposal authorities but transferring the water conservation and water quality functions of river authorities to the Regional Water Authorities.

299. We do not see any advantage in attempting to summarise this part of our report, or the subsequent discussion of the considerations to be taken into account in reaching decisions about future organisation. The descriptions of the alternative systems of organisation stand by themselves. Chapter 8 is quite brief, and to quote particular sentences out of context would be misleading and result in distortions.

300. There is, however, one point in this part of our report to which we should like to give further emphasis. We are all convinced that the Regional Water Authorities must be strong bodies. It is essential that there should be a much greater degree of co-ordination than exists at present, and it is only through the establishment of strong regional bodies that this can be brought about. The differences between us are not on this point, but on the subsidiary question of the best way in which this objective can be achieved.

301. The principal conclusions and recommendations contained in the remainder of our report are as follows.

302. *The problems to be faced.* Meeting the increasing demand for water in England and Wales constitutes a major problem (paras. 102-5). Since the publication of the Proudman Report in 1962, considerable advances have been made in overall planning. The importance of national planning has become increasingly apparent (paras. 106-10).

303. At the same time it has become apparent that there will have to be a much greater reuse of water in nearly all parts of the country, and therefore a much greater concern with the treatment given to water after use (paras. 111-15). The effective promotion of a policy of reuse will depend upon the existence of a single, comprehensive water management plan for every river basin, which includes water reclamation (paras. 116-19).

304. It is technically possible to cope with the increased use of water, but the solutions also have to be publicly acceptable and make the minimum demand on resources (paras. 120-1).

305. Quite apart from questions of organisation, the existing legislation is capable of detailed improvement and we have assumed that such improvements will in any case be made (paras. 122-4).

306. There should be a sweeping reduction in the number of separate operating units in sewage disposal, and a further reduction in the number of separate operating units in water supply, in each case to a number significantly lower than one hundred. The optimum number of river authorities depends upon the exact functions they will be expected to perform in future (paras. 125-30).

307. At present there are increasing conflicts of interest between the various authorities and inadequate mechanisms for resolving them, apart from intervention by central government (para. 131). The most important areas of conflicts are (i) inflexibility in the use of existing resources (paras. 132-3), (ii) divided responsibility for new sources (paras. 134-8), (iii) the promotion of joint or national schemes (paras. 140-4), (iv) conflicts of interest in regard to water reclamation (para. 145). There are also wider conflicts which have to be kept in mind between our objectives in relation to water and wider social objectives (paras. 146-7).

308. In addition to detailed improvements in legislation and reductions in the number of units, the relationship between the various authorities must be changed so that comprehensive water management plans can be drawn up and so that, once such plans have been agreed, the system of organisation and the financial arrangements permit their implementation (para. 148). At the same time it must be borne in mind that if a body is under a statutory obligation to supply water, then either it must itself have the powers to enable it to meet this obligation, or there must be another body which has a statutory obligation to make water available to it (para. 139).

309. *The improvement of planning and co-ordination.* A long-term national plan is already in preparation but its scope should be widened to cover all the relevant aspects of water management (paras. 149-52). It should form the basis for a Green Paper on national water policy so that, after public debate and any consequential modifications, the chosen strategy becomes a firm general commitment of government policy (para. 153).

310. In order to ensure the effective programming of capital works in accordance with the national plan there must be five-year action programmes (para. 154-6). These should cover a wider range of projects than the national plan (para. 157). The responsibility for compiling them and supervising their implementation should be given to a number of Regional Water Authorities, the right number probably lying between six and fifteen (paras. 158-61).

311. The Regional Water Authority would also draw up a long-term water plan for the region within the framework of the national water plan and regional land-use policies (paras. 162-4).

312. This kind of planning and co-ordination would be a largely new function, but it is as important as the individual functions of water supply, sewage disposal and river management (para. 165-6). One necessary and

desirable consequence of it is that a capital project would be competing for finance only against other projects in the water field, and not as now against projects in connection with other local authority services (para. 167).

313. *Organisation at the national level.* We have not considered in detail the form of organisation at the national level. But we envisage that there will be a body corresponding to the present Water Resources Board, and its field of work ought to be extended to include all the relevant aspects of water management (para. 246-7). We also think that in view of the size and complexity of some of the schemes now under consideration, this national body ought to be constituted with a reserve power to acquire, construct, own and operate water conservation works itself, which if necessary could be activated by an Order made by the relevant minister (paras. 248-58).

314. *The position of Wales.* The conclusions and recommendations elsewhere in our report apply equally to England and to Wales (para. 259). We foresee insuperable difficulties in involving another statutory body directly in the construction and operation of reservoirs, as proposed by the Welsh Council (para. 264). However, a body corresponding to the present Welsh Committee of the Water Resources Board could play a useful part in the consideration of Welsh problems (para. 266).

## ACKNOWLEDGMENTS

315. We should like to thank all those who helped us by giving evidence, both written and oral. We should also like to thank our Assessors, who not only helped us to assess the evidence but provided us with numerous special studies which were of the greatest assistance to us. We also record our grateful thanks to our Secretariat, who have carried an exceptionally heavy load, and who have maintained an admirable service throughout the whole of our inquiry.

A. H. WILSON  (*Chairman*)
J. B. BENNETT
JOHN COCKRAM
DE RAMSEY
E. A. DREW
W. M. FERRIER
HUGH FISH
J. O. GRIEVES
D. F. GRIFFITHS
A. E. HALL
B. J. HALLIDAY
T. R. B. HENCHLEY
R. LEG HETHERINGTON
GEORGE HOWARD
JOHN LL. HUGHES
C. J. JACKSON
HAROLD LAMBERT
FRANK LAW
R. J. LILLICRAP

W. H. MULLEY
NUGENT
G. C. OGDEN
J. L. ROUGHTON
M. G. SIMPSON
G. SOLT
R. E. WOODWARD

4th February 1971.

# APPENDIX 1

## LIST OF BODIES AND INDIVIDUALS WHO SUBMITTED EVIDENCE

These bodies which submitted oral evidence are asterisked and the names of the witnesses are given.

PUBLIC CORPORATIONS AND OFFICIAL BODIES

British Transport Docks Board.
* British Waterways Board.
  WITNESSES: Mr D. G. McCance, Mr A. Blenkharn, Mr A. J. Brawn, Mr P. R. Lisle, Mr T. T. Luckcuck, Mr H. C. Rutherfurd.

* Central Electricity Generating Board.
  WITNESS: Mr E. J. Pipe.

Consumer Council.
Countryside Commission.
Port of London Authority.
Water Pollution Research Laboratory.

* Welsh Council.
  WITNESSES: Prof. Brinley Thomas, Lt. Col. the Hon. R. E. B. Beaumont, Prof. Ivor Gowan, Mr R. H. Williams.

LOCAL AUTHORITIES

* Association of Municipal Corporations.
  WITNESSES: Ald. G. F. Hickson, Mr J. F. Finch, Mr E. J. O. Gardiner, Mr D. B. Harrison, Mr P. Hodgson, Mr W. G. H. Tripp.

* County Councils Association.
  WITNESSES: Col. G. P. Shakerley, Mr C. P. H. McCall, Mr J. Westoll, Mr. A. C. Hetherington, Mr G. Matthews.

* Rural District Councils Association.
  WITNESSES: Dr A. Robinson Thomas, Mr W. Charlesworth, Mr W. Phillips, Dr J. S. Robertson, Mr A. S. Watts, Mr S. Rhodes, Mr R. Mewett.

* Urban District Councils Association.
  WITNESSES: Mr H. Brummitt, Mr F. Barnes, Mr R. Warrington.

Welsh Counties Committee.

Coventry CBC.
Greater London Council.
Manchester CBC.

Peak Park Planning Board.

Brightlingsea UDC.

## RIVER AUTHORITIES

\* Association of River Authorities.
>    WITNESSES: Mr S. H. J. Bates, Sir Wm. Dugdale Bt., Mr D. J. Kinner-
>    sley.

Cornwall RA.
East Suffolk and Norfolk RA (jointly with Lincolnshire RA).
Essex RA.
Hampshire RA.
Lee Conservancy Catchment Board.
Lincolnshire RA (jointly with East Suffolk and Norfolk RA).
Mersey and Weaver RA.
Northumbrian RA.
Sussex RA.
Thames Conservancy.
Trent RA.
Welland and Nene RA.

## WATER UNDERTAKERS

\* British Waterworks Association.
>    WITNESSES: Mr S. G. Barrett, Ald. G. W. G. Fitzsimons, Ald. Dr.
>    L. Glass, Lt. Col. A. Jardine, Mr R. W. Melvin, Mr L.
>    Millis, Mr E. Round.

Water Companies Association.

Bucks Water Board.

Cotswold Water Board.
Coventry CBC.
Craven Water Board.

Derwent Valley Water Board.
Doncaster and District Joint Water Board.
Durham County Water Board.

East Shropshire Water Board.
East Yorkshire (Wolds Area) Water Board.

Fylde Water Board.

Lune Valley Water Board.

Mid-Sussex Water Company.
Manchester CBC.

Northallerton and the Dales Water Board.
North West Gloucestershire Water Board.
North West Sussex Water Board.
North Wilts Water Board.

Oxfordshire and District Water Board.

River Dove Water Board.
Rugby Joint Water Board.

Wakefield and District Water Board.
West Somerset Water Board.

PROFESSIONAL ASSOCIATIONS, TRADE UNIONS, ETC.

Association of Public Health Inspectors.
Association of Rural District Council Surveyors.
Association of Waterworks Chemists and Bacteriologists.

Institute of Biology.
Institute of Municipal Treasurers and Accountants.
* Institute of Water Pollution Control.
    WITNESSES: Mr H. H. Stanbridge, Mr V. H. Lewin, Mr C. Lumb,
    Mr R. Wood.

* Institution of Civil Engineers.
    WITNESSES: Mr J. T. Calvert, Mr G. McLeod, Mr D. J. D. Clark.

Institution of Municipal Engineers.
* Institution of Public Health Engineers.
    WITNESSES: Mr W. A. Feather, Mr K. Guiver,
    Mr P. G. Spencer, Mr I. B. Muirhead.

* Institution of Water Engineers.
    WITNESSES: Mr A. E. Guild, Mr M. Nixon, Dr A. T. Palin,
    Mr G. M. Swales, Mr A. C. Twort, Mr J. P. Banbury.

National and Local Government Officers Association.
River authority branches of the National and Local Government Officers
Association.
National Union of Public Employees.
National Union of Water Works Employees.

Royal Institute of Public Health and Hygiene.
Royal Society of Health.

* Society for Water Treatment and Examination.
    WITNESSES: Dr R. F. Packham, Dr N. P. Burman, Mr W. M. Lewis.

Society of Chemical Industry.
Society of Clerks of Water Boards.
Society of Medical Officers of Health.

TRADE ASSOCIATIONS

Brewers Society.
British Leather Federation.
British Paper and Board Makers Association.
British Textile Employers Association.
British Water and Effluent Treatment Plant Association.
Chemical Industries Association.

* Confederation of British Industry.
    WITNESSES: Mr H. C. I. Rogers, Mr G. W. Cook, Mr P. S. G. Flint,
                Mr H. E. Hopthrow, Mr A. I. Biggs, Mr E. M. Felgate,
                Mr P. S. Taylor.

Cooling Water Association.
Country Landowners Association.

National Farmers Union.
National Federation of Building Trade Employers.

AMENITY ASSOCIATIONS

* Committee for Environmental Conservation.
    WITNESS: Mr F. D. Corbin.

Council for the Protection of Rural England.
National Anglers Council.
National Federation of Anglers.
Salmon and Trout Association.

OTHER BODIES

Association of Drainage Authorities.
* Association of Joint Sewerage Boards.
    WITNESSES: Coun. D. R. Bull, Mr T. N. Cockroft, Mr J. H. Pawley,
                Mr D. A. D. Reeve.

Dock and Harbour Authorities Association.
Oil and Water Industries Working Group.
Water Research Association.

Mr Delwyn Davies.
Mr F. Charles Greenfield.
Coun. W. J. McKechin.
Mr C. N. Matthews.
Coun. Charles H. de Peyer.
Mr E. Horsfall Turner.

# APPENDIX 2

## WATER QUALITY

### Note by the Directorate of Engineering of the Department of the Environment.

#### I. HISTORY OF THE RIVER POLLUTION PROBLEM AND THE GROWTH OF CONTROL

1. In the early part of the nineteenth century sewage disposal by the water-borne system simply meant moving sewage and refuse from the streets and depositing it in the nearest watercourse. The scale of the problem was altered however during the Industrial Revolution by the migration of population from the rural areas to the towns and by the establishment of factories on the rivers, where there was a supply of water for power and industrial processes. The uncontrolled discharge of sewage and solid and liquid industrial wastes gradually turned many of the country's rivers into open sewers, particularly in the industrial North, in the Midlands and in the London area. It is alleged that even navigation through locks on the Thames was impeded by surface accumulation of sewage.

2. The grave danger to health this produced led to the passing of the Public Health Act 1875 and the Rivers Pollution Prevention Act 1876 and for more than half a century these two acts formed the basic legislation governing sewerage, sewage treatment and pollution control. The next major step forward was the appointment in 1898 of the Royal Commission on Sewage Disposal. Between 1901 and 1915 the Commission produced a series of reports which were to be the foundation for sewage treatment practice for many decades: they recommended a general standard for the quality of sewage works effluents from inland towns, which stipulated upper limits on suspended solids and biochemical oxygen demand (BOD), and it became normal practice to design works to produce a 'Royal Commission effluent' with the avoidance of nuisance as the main objective. Earlier legislation on Public Health was consolidated in the Public Health Act 1936, in which the powers and responsibilities for the provision of sewage treatment are laid down.

3. Up to that time main drainage had generally been restricted to the more urban areas. Many rural areas were without a public water supply, their water consumption was therefore very low, and the absence of modern waterborne sanitation gave some protection to the rivers, although they were not entirely immune from pollution by discharges of sink waste and crude sewage. After the 1939-45 war however there was a steady change in condi-

tions in the rural areas, stimulated by legislation which gave financial assistance towards the provision of water supplies and main drainage, and many watercourses began to receive discharges of sewage effluent for the first time.

4. Under the River Boards Act 1948 river boards were established and under the Rivers (Prevention of Pollution) Act 1951 they were given improved powers to control river pollution, mainly by the control of new discharges to non-tidal waters. Subsequent legislation gave them control over new discharges to tidal estuaries and over pre-1951 discharges to non-tidal and certain tidal waters. The Water Resources Act 1963 transferred these powers to the new river authorities.

5. Control has generally been exercised by stipulating conditions with which polluting discharges must comply and so far as sewage effluent is concerned it has been common practice to require treatment to Royal Commission Standard. Over the years however increases in water consumption have led to considerable increases in the volume of effluents discharged to rivers. At the same time the need to provide the additional water has led to increased abstractions from many rivers, to a reduction in the natural flow of clean water, and thus to a diminution in the quality and quantity of water available for the dilution of effluents. As a consequence of these changed conditions and a better understanding of the chemistry and biology of rivers there has been a tendency towards the fairly frequent imposition of standards more restrictive than those of the Royal Commission. This policy has had the support of the ministry in cases where it was shown to be justified and the ministry have in fact issued a memorandum giving guidance to river authorities and sewage disposal authorities on the subject.[1]

6. Although the same controls apply to the direct discharge of industrial effluents to rivers they can often be more difficult to enforce, because of such factors as the cost of treatment (which could adversely affect the cost of the product) or a lack of the space necessary for an adequate treatment plant. A situation could arise where the only alternative to the continuance of a highly polluting industrial discharge would be the closure of the factory. There are also many hundreds of discharges of highly polluting farm waste, which are particularly difficult to control because of their scattered distribution. The ministry have also issued guidance on standards for industrial effluents.[2]

II. SOURCES OF POLLUTION AND THEIR EFFECTS

7. The most common source of pollution is sewage. This may be solely of domestic origin, solely of industrial origin or, frequently, a mixture of both. Domestic sewage is fairly consistent in composition and comprises about 99.9 per cent of water and 0.1 per cent of organic and inorganic matter in solution and in suspension.

1 Ministry of Housing and Local Government. Technical problems of river authorities and sewage disposal authorities in laying down and complying with limits of quality for effluents more restrictive than those of the Royal Commission. HMSO, 1966.
2 Ministry of Housing and Local Government. Standards of effluents to rivers with particular reference to industrial effluents. HMSO, 1968.

8. In the normal sewage treatment processes the suspended solids are reduced mainly by settlement to a limit acceptable for discharge. Purification of organic matter, consisting mainly of compounds of carbon and of nitrogen, is effected by oxidation, which takes place in the presence of atmospheric oxygen by the action of micro-organisms, carbon being oxidised to carbon dioxide and (usually) nitrogen being oxidised to nitrate. In certain cases however some unoxidised nitrogen remains in the effluent in the form of ammonia. Oxidation is not complete and the BOD of the effluent is an indication of the residual oxidisable organic matter.

9. The residual unoxidised impurities in the effluent are capable of further oxidation in the river. River water usually contains oxygen dissolved from the air and the micro-organisms naturally present in the water cause the residual oxidisable impurities to consume some of this oxygen. No harmful consequences will follow if the consumption of oxygen by the residual impurities does not make undue demands upon the oxygen available in the river and the additional oxygen which the river can absorb from the atmosphere. This natural process is often referred to as 'self-purification'. Where an undue demand is made on the oxygen resources however the dissolved oxygen in the river may fall to a level insufficient to support fish life. Even greater demands for oxygen may reduce the dissolved oxygen to zero, and this condition can be accompanied by an unsightly appearance and the foul odours associated with putrefaction, which have often been encountered in rivers flowing through industrial areas.

10. Sewage contains dissolved mineral matter including sodium chloride (common salt). This is unaffected by sewage treatment, is passed to the stream unchanged and can have an important bearing on the suitability of a stream as a source of potable water.

11. All domestic sewage can contain, and must be presumed to contain at times, pathogenic bacteria responsible for water-borne disease. While a large proportion of the organisms are removed by sewage treatment very large numbers remain in the treated effluents and must be removed by any abstractors who use that river as a source of potable water.

12. The liquid wastes of industry vary enormously in nature and composition, and many industrial wastes are not dissimilar to domestic sewage in their general content. Notable in this group are the waste products from food and drink manufacture and to a lesser extent other industries such as paper, leather and textiles where the raw materials are of animal or vegetable origin. Such wastes can be largely purified by the basic processes of settlement and biological oxidation to produce an effluent having an effect on the river similar to that of domestic sewage effluent of comparable strength. The use of chemicals in some industrial processes however can result in the effluent having more harmful effects. There may also be a substantial discharge of non-oxidisable impurities and these too can have an important bearing on the condition of the river and its suitability as a source of public water supply.

13. Effluents from the metal-finishing industries are marked by compounds such as cyanides, heavy metals and chromium, which are toxic to fish and to

93

man in relatively small quantities. It is a vital part of pollution control to ensure that the concentration of these compounds is reduced to an acceptably low level of treatment of the effluents. Industries engaged in the manufacture of chemicals and those using chemicals in their processes also produce effluents that can be harmful in various ways and to varying degrees but it is not possible to generalise about their effects because of the great variety of substances involved.

14. The increased use of agricultural fertilisers and pesticides has introduced a problem because residues soak into the ground and increase the concentration of mineral salts (including nitrates) in rivers. This factor may be significant when considering the use of a river as a source of potable water.

15. Heated effluents from industry and in particular from direct-cooled electricity generating stations, even if they are pure in other respects, can influence the effects of polluting substances already present in the river. The rate of oxygen depletion will be increased and raising the temperature of the river may have a distinct effect on animal and plant life. It is now the practice, however, to install cooling towers at new river-side power stations. This reduces the amount of heat entering the river and also provides a beneficial effect by way of oxygenation, but evaporation does increase the concentration of dissolved solids.

16. Probably the greatest potential risk from industry is from accidental discharges and public attention has recently been directed to the consequences of such 'accidents'. This is an ever-present risk and to prevent it entirely would be almost impossible.

17. Often industrial effluents can with advantage be treated in admixture with domestic sewage and pollution control authorities generally do their utmost to encourage the discharge of industrial effluents to sewers rather than direct to rivers. However some industrial effluents can seriously inhibit biological oxidation and other processes in normal sewage treatment and in extreme cases can lead to a complete breakdown of the plant.

18. Brief mention has been made of the suspended solids in effluents. If these are composed of organic matter they can make demands on the oxygen in the river; they can adversely affect the river through the deposition of sludge and silt, especially if the flow is sluggish.

19. Public attention tends to be drawn mainly to the pollution of rivers but there is a growing risk of the contamination of underground water through the seepage of rainwater which has been in contact with fertilisers or with waste tips or with harmful waste chemicals spread on the ground. Although the Water Resources Act 1963 gave river authorities control over the disposal of wastes into underground strata by way of boreholes they have no powers to control or prevent contamination by seepage.

III. THE GENERAL STATE OF THE RIVERS

20. An informal survey which was carried out by the ministry in 1958 and covered some 20,000 miles of non-tidal rivers in England and Wales showed

that about 73 per cent of river miles were in Class 1 (unpolluted or recovered from pollution), 15 per cent in Class 2 (of doubtful quality and needing improvement), 6 per cent in Class 3 (poor quality) and 6 per cent in Class 4 (grossly polluted and incapable of supporting fish life).[1] Whilst these figures do not seem to be unduly alarming at first glance they mean that some 2,500 miles of river were in a poor or grossly polluted state. Moreover the situation in certain industrial areas such as the North West and the Midlands was much worse than the national average.

21. There are some 5,000 sewage disposal works in England and Wales and despite the large annual expenditure many of these are making unsatisfactory discharges. The situation is generally considered to be better than it was in 1958 but many stretches of river are still in a grossly polluted state.

22. A full picture of the present state of the rivers will be available later this year on the completion of a river pollution survey which is being carried out by the ministry with the co-operation of the river authorities and the CBI but meanwhile some information on the situation in industrial areas can be obtained from the annual reports of the relevant river authorities. For example, the latest report of the Mersey and Weaver River Authority shows that the principal rivers are classed as either 'bad' or 'very bad' from as far inland as Rochdale and Oldham right down through Manchester to the estuary and the latest report of the Trent River Authority shows that for most of their length the principal rivers from as far inland as Wolverhampton, down through Birmingham and Nottingham are in a comparable condition.

## IV.  PARTIES WITH AN INTEREST IN WATER QUALITY

23. The prime use of water is for the maintenance of healthy human life and therefore where water is abstracted for public supply the supply undertaker must be the party with the most important interest. Industry as the largest user of water also has a particular interest, especially as the quality of water required by different industrial processes varies so widely. There are however many other uses of, and interests in, water which must be given their place in any consideration of quality.

24. Riparian owners and occupiers have an interest because under common law it is their right to have the water flow past their land without sensible alteration in its natural quality. Farmers will often want the water to be suitable for irrigation and cattle-watering. Commercial salmon-fishing interests require the rivers and estuaries to be clean enough for the ascent of spawning fish and the seaward migration of their progeny, and trout farmers need clean water for their commercial undertakings.

25. The interests of individuals go further however. Because of increased leisure and the mobility provided by the motor car the public at large use the rivers for recreational purposes in increasing numbers. The variety of recreational uses is too extensive to list in detail, but angling, sailing and bathing immediately come to mind, plus all the pastimes associated with 'a day by

1  Ministry of Housing and Local Government and Welsh Office, Working Party on Sewage Disposal. **Taken for Granted,** pp. 14-15 and table 1.

the river'. People in boats do not want to sail in water that looks like sewage, nor do they want to churn up foul-smelling sludge or silt when they start the engine of a power boat. And bathers and participants in water sports want to be sure that there are no risks to health as a consequence of immersion in or contact with river water.

26. Anglers deplore any tendency towards the sort of deterioration in water quality which leads to fish mortality or a reduction in fish numbers. Deterioration in a good river can happen quickly through the accidental discharge of toxic wastes; or it can be brought about by the onset of drought conditions, which leave insufficient dilution for normally acceptable effluents; or it can be the result of a variety of other factors affecting the chemical and biological condition of the river.

## V.   THE PARTICULAR INTEREST OF THE ABSTRACTOR AND THE CONSUMER

27. The tendency towards the increasing use for public supply of water taken from the more heavily polluted lower reaches of rivers is a cause for some concern.   In order to understand why it is necessary to know something about water analysis as an indicator of quality.

28. Sewage treatment effects a large percentage removal of the dissolved organic compounds originally present in the raw sewage but a certain amount of 'hard' organic matter remains.   This is not amenable to biological oxidation in the river, and is not reduced to any important extent by the normal processes of water treatment.   If therefore the raw water contains treated sewage residues the water passed into supply after treatment will contain residual organic matter.   Analysis of the water by standard determinations will give an indication of the concentration of these residues but will throw no light on the identity of the compounds present.

29. More refined methods of analysis are continually being developed but at the present time and in the foreseeable future it will not be possible to identify all the large number of complicated organic substances which may be present.   Most of the substances derived from domestic sewage are probably harmless since these residues have been consumed by human beings for a long time.   However the water may also contain hard organic residues from industrial processes, which will be 'concealed' analytically by the other organic residues and may have a significance for health.   It is of course possible to reduce all organic residues considerably by additional and expensive methods of water treatment but it is not possible to eliminate them entirely.

30. It is important to realise that many industries, particularly chemical production industries, may not know what substances are present in their waste products.   Indeed the analysis of this waste, other than in general terms, may be as difficult as the analysis of the residues in water supplies. The problems can be intensified by a progressive build-up of undesirable residues in river basins where water is used several times on its journey to the sea.

31. To summarise, the protection of the sources of raw water from pollution still remains the best method available to a water undertaker to ensure that the water supplied to the public is, as the law requires, 'wholesome'.

32. Industry's largest requirement for water is for cooling in which quality considerations are not so important. Another extensive use of water by industry in which quality may not be very important is the transport of materials through the manufacturing process, for example in the manufacture of china clay and cement. Another good example is the production of paper from imported wood-pulp, which basically consists of the addition of water to the raw material and its subsequent removal.

33. Many processes in such industries as food production and brewing can be adequately served by the normal public supply.

34. The textile industry generally requires soft water and has often located itself in areas where this is naturally available. In other areas artificial softening has sometimes been carried out by the supply undertaking for the benefit of the industry.

35. At the extreme there are some industrial operations which require water of a high degree of purity that does not exist naturally and is not available from any public supply. These industries include the manufacture of electronic devices, pharmaceuticals and the many industries which require ultra-pure water for high-pressure boiler feed. In all these cases it is necessary for the user himself to treat the water in order to make it suitable for his particular purpose.

36. There is an increasing use of river water for the spray irrigation of crops and there must be certain hazards attached to this when the raw water is polluted. Plants and soil can be harmfully affected by an excess of such substances as boron, sodium and toxic metals.

VI.   THE MANAGEMENT OF RIVER WATER QUALITY

37. At the present time the quality of a particular stretch of river is influenced by the activities of several parties. Local authorities (or occasionally joint sewerage boards) are responsible for providing sewage treatment of the domestic and industrial wastes discharged to the sewers. The river authority has the power to lay down the conditions with which effluents must comply. Industrialists who discharge their effluents direct to rivers are responsible for providing the treatment necessary to meet the river authority's requirements. The water undertaker influences the quality of the river because his abstractions alter the flow. River authorities can carry out works to control and divert rivers with advantageous results.

38. It is probably true to say that the greatest single influence on the location of sewage treatment works in the past has been topography. Having once collected the sewage an authority would generally site its treatment works close to the nearest watercourse which offered reasonable dilution, and that is where the effluent would be discharged. At best the effluent pipe might have been extended if there were a water intake a short distance downstream, but little consideration if any would have been given to the river basin as a whole.

39. If water quality is to be properly managed, it may in the short term be necessary to decide what is to be the prime function of each stretch of

river and to attach to it a quality standard appropriate to that function. Some stretches will be required as sources of water for public supply, but it is clear that not all rivers or parts of rivers will be suitable for, or required for, this purpose. Different considerations can be applied to those that are not. Some rivers may even be considered as unlikely to support fish in the foreseeable future. Others may be considered useful for all forms of recreation including fishing. It is possible to foresee therefore a number of defined states of quality for rivers or parts of a river.

40. Many of the factors that affect quality are interrelated in a complicated way and it will not be easy to achieve the optimal integration. Abstraction of water may worsen conditions downstream by reducing the amount of water available to dilute any effluent discharged: the return of a purified effluent at a point upstream of the intake from which the water was originally abstracted could improve some characteristics of the river by improving the dilution, but could equally well cause a deterioration through a build-up of dissolved salts. Computer techniques however have now made it possible to evaluate the overall effect of varying all the relevant parameters including the location, quantity and quality of discharges and abstractions. A study of this type is already under way in the catchment of the River Trent.

41. A time may come when the optimal use of a river cannot be achieved without some radical alteration in the long-established pattern of abstractions and discharges. It might become necessary to prohibit the large-scale development of particular industries in certain river basins which are economical sources of high-quality water. On the other hand it might be necessary to use water abstracted from certain stretches for non-potable supplies only. This would have the effect of releasing the equivalent amount of better quality water for domestic supplies and it would seem to be a maxim of good management that no consumer should be supplied with water of a higher quality than he reasonably requires.

42. The sort of problems that will have to be examined are:

   a. What advantages would there be in grouping discharges or spreading them out?

   b. Would it be better to discharge at Point A with an effluent of a given quality or at Point B with an effluent of a different quality?

   c. What standard of quality is to be attached to a particular stretch of river having regard to all its uses?

   d. How much water has to be potable, and to what extent could the distribution of water of different qualities meet everyone's needs and benefit the river basin?

   e. In what areas do quality requirements play a major part in influencing planning and what steps have to be taken in these areas to maintain quality?

# APPENDIX 3

## NOTE ON DIFFICULTIES OVER THE BUILDING OF NEW RESERVOIRS

1. One of the main difficulties which water undertakers and river authorities are facing at the moment is that of obtaining authorisation for new reservoirs, and this is a matter of great concern to those responsible for ensuring continued supplies of water. If we include the potential contribution of estuarine barrages, of desalination and of the increased reuse of water, and make full allowance for the increased yields that can be obtained by more sophisticated use of existing sources, it will still be necessary to construct a number of new reservoirs if we are to survive even the seventies safely, much less to the end of the century.

2. Some water schemes would involve the construction of reservoirs in National Parks, and this would in some instances lead to a loss of amenity. If so, the extent of the loss has to be weighed carefully against the loss that would be caused by alternative courses of action. For example the construction of a barrage will have repercussions on the character and ecology of an estuary. Reservoirs in lowland areas may affect very valuable agricultural land. Excessive abstractions of underground water would diminish the flows in streams and rivers, or even cause them to dry up entirely. If large numbers of desalination plants were to be constructed, sites for them might well have to be found on hitherto undeveloped stretches of coast. The increased reuse of water might necessitate the construction of extensive new treatment works on the fringes of the main urban areas.

3. On the other hand the construction of reservoirs may involve gains to amenity as well as losses. England and Wales are not naturally well endowed with inland lakes. Perhaps as a result of this there has not in the past been as much participation in water-based recreation as in some other countries. But the demand for facilities for water-based sports is now growing rapidly and the multi-purpose use of reservoirs is one of the main methods available to satisfy this demand. As well as facilities for water-based sport, reservoirs already provide enjoyment on a large scale through their bird and fish populations, and give a no less real pleasure to countless people merely as a landscape feature. All proposals for new reservoirs should take full account of amenity aspects and in suitable cases include facilities for recreation.

4. Why are these points so often overlooked, and why has there been such opposition towards reservoirs? We believe that a large part of the answer lies in two factors: lack of effective public relations; and inadequate compensation for the acquisition of land, loss of livelihood and disturbance.

5. One of the criticisms most often made of reservoir proposals is that they are part of a piecemeal approach to meeting the increased demand for water. We believe that the publication of a Green Paper on national water policy, which we have recommended in para. 153, will help to solve this problem by bringing before a wider public the concepts and choices involved in national water resources planning. Regional plans ought also to be placed before the widest possible public and it may be desirable to produce popular versions of

them for this purpose. The wider understanding of the objectives and methods of water management which we hope this will induce is a necessary condition for a more favourable general attitude towards the activities of water authorities.

6. As for the second factor we mentioned above, compensation, it was suggested to us that the compensation given when agricultural land is acquired for a reservoir is inadequate, particularly when viewed against the difficulty of a farmer in reinstating himself on an equivalent holding. The cost of land acquired for reservoirs and works is a small proportion of the total cost of schemes. Delays can, through escalation of costs, be much more expensive than any increase in land costs arising from increased compensation, but are inevitable when the level of payments is felt to be inequitable. Clearly compensation is a technical subject on which we as a Committee are not qualified to express an opinion. We also appreciate that the question of compensation for land acquired for reservoirs cannot be viewed in isolation from other compensation arrangements. We understand, however, that a general review of compensation is now in progress, and we would urge on the Secretary of State the desirability of taking steps which will alleviate the anxieties and sense of injustice which often seem to exist at present.

## APPENDIX 4

## EXCHEQUER GRANTS AND THE FINANCING OF SEWERAGE AND SEWAGE DISPOSAL

### Note by the Department of the Environment

I. RURAL WATER SUPPLIES AND SEWERAGE GRANTS

1. The justification for rural water supplies and sewerage grants is that, because development is less dense in rural areas, longer runs of pipe are required in proportion to the number of properties served either with mains water or main drainage. Below a specified cost per property, the exchequer pays 35 per cent of the amount by which the cost of the sewerage or the water distribution network exceeds a notional urban cost. Where an exchequer grant is made the county council is obliged to make a grant: where agreement cannot be reached on the amount of the county council's grant this is determined by the minister. County councils commonly match the exchequer grant.

2. By the end of 1970, the exchequer share of the cost of schemes approved since the second world war in England and Wales amounted to £33.4m for water supply and £66.2m for sewerage. These are capital figures but most grants are paid by instalments of principal and interest over full loan periods. The awards for the calendar year 1970 were £0.61m for water supply and £5.51m for sewerage, illustrating the near completion of the water programme while the sewerage programme continues at a substantial rate because sewerage naturally follows later.

3. The future of all grants to local authorities is to be reviewed in connection with the reorganisation of local government, and those in support of rural water supplies and sewerage would need to be considered in the context of the future system of exchequer aid to local government. A Green Paper is expected later this year. In their present context the grants may be regarded as primarily promotional (main drainage at a cost to the rural district of only one-third the cash price); or primarily redistributive, meeting part of the cost out of central government taxation which is supposedly more equitable than the rates (though some of it is certainly more regressive). Perhaps the distinction is unreal. Because it keeps the consequent increase in rate poundage within what the authority subjectively considers to be practicable, the grant makes it more likely that rural water supplies will be provided by the water undertaker (sometimes on condition that the rural district council make up the undertaker's income from the extension to an economic level during an initial period of years), and that rural sewerage will be provided by the district council.

4. If reorganisation produces large units, the spreading of the higher cost of rural services over a mixed urban and rural area will reduce the effect on rate poundage and to that extent make grant less necessary. On the other hand there could be a reluctance on the part of the authority to spend on a scheme which, in proportion to its cost, would benefit relatively few people, and the grant could still be needed for its promotional aspects.

## II. RATE SUPPORT GRANT

5. The system of exchequer grants in aid of the revenue expenditure of local authorities was changed by the Local Government Act 1966. Under that Act the minister is required to determine the aggregate amount of such grants for each of the next two or more years after taking account of the expected level of 'relevant expenditure' by local authorities in those years. Relevant expenditure is defined to exclude expenditure on local authorities' own housing and on trading services, such as water, but covers expenditure on sewerage and sewage disposal (including loan charges) and also payments under precept to, among others, river authorities.

6. An an administrative decision, the aggregate of the revenue grants is determined at a percentage of relevant expenditure: 57½ per cent for 1971/2 and 58 per cent for 1972/73. (The percentage has increased each year since the commencement of the system.)

7. The estimated relevant expenditure for 1971/72 was £3,795.4m, including £142.9m for sewerage and sewage disposal. The aggregate amount of exchequer grants for that year was accordingly determined at £2,182m (57½ per cent of £3,795m). These estimates reflect prices ruling at November 1970 and may be increased to take account of subsequent movements in pay and prices.

8. From the aggregate of exchequer grants there is deducted the estimated amounts of specific grants for the respective years in respect of revenue expenditure. (The major items are police, magistrates courts and legal aid, improvements grants, and rate rebates, together accounting for £139m out

101

of a total of £178m in 1971/72; but the rural sewerage grants of ...£4m are also in the total.) The balance is the aggregate of the rate support grant.

9. The rate grant is distributed in three parts:

    (i) a domestic element (£117m in 1971/72), paid to rating authorities to compensate them for the rate poundage differential in favour of domestic ratepayers ($9\frac{1}{2}$p in the £ in 1971/2);

    (ii) a resources element (£280m); and

    (iii) a needs element (the balance, of £1,607m) distributed to county and county borough councils broadly speaking on the basis of weighted population.

The resources element is payable to any county, county borough or county district council in whose area a penny rate produces less per head of population than the national average. It is a percentage grant payable on all expenditure which would otherwise fall upon the rates and the percentage is calculated so as, in effect, to bring the rate resources up to the national average.

10. Individual local authorities qualify for widely different percentages of the resources element of the rate support grant. These vary locally from nothing to about 70 per cent but average about 13.4 per cent.

11. Although the deficit on a local authority's water account charged to the general rate does not enter in the determination of the aggregate of exchequer grants, it too earns a share of the rate resources element and so affects the distribution, but not the total amount, of the rate support grant. (In 1967/68 there was a deficit of about £4.2m met out of the general rates.)

12. The contribution which the rate support grant makes to the financing of sewerage and sewage disposal is a matter of definition. Before the establishment of the present grant system the only exchequer grant apart from the rural sewerage grant which was generally available and could be said to go towards the cost of sewerage and sewage disposal was the rate deficiency grant, the equivalent of the resources element of the present rate support grant, which was calculated in a similar way. The needs element replaces certain specific grants and the general grant, which in turn replaced specific grants for certain services. The specific grants that were replaced did not include any towards the cost of sewerage or sewage disposal. At the same time the needs element represents more than the grants it replaced, because it includes residual amounts to allow for any part of the annual increase in overall grant percentage that may not be taken up otherwise, for example through the domestic element.

13. If the responsibility for sewage disposal and certain sewers were to be transferred to bodies other than local authorities, and the cost of these services were to be met by charges rather than by a precept, then the users of these services would lose whatever assistance they may at present be regarded as deriving in that particular capacity from the rate support grant. And the charges paid would be larger in aggregate than what they would otherwise have paid through the general rate, by the amount of that assistance.

14. Whether the users of these services as a class would on balance suffer any loss however is a more difficult question. The answer would depend on the repercussions which the change had on the level of exchequer assistance to local authorities. This assistance is being reviewed at present in the context of local government reform, and it is impossible to predict with any certainty therefore what the repercussions would be. If we assume for the moment however that exchequer assistance will continue in its present form, taking sewage disposal and certain sewers away from local authorities would reduce the level of 'relevant expenditure' on which decisions on the aggregate amount of exchequer assistance are based. It would then be for the government of the day to decide as a matter of policy how to react to this situation. Exchequer assistance might be maintained at the absolute level which it would otherwise have reached, so increasing the percentage of 'relevant expenditure' met by the exchequer; or exchequer assistance might be maintained at the same proportion of the lower absolute level of 'relevant expenditure'; or in certain circumstances (for example if other local taxes were being established alongside rates) the proportion of 'relevant expenditure' met by exchequer assistance might be reduced.

15. Even if on balance there were to be no change in the overall position of the users of sewerage and sewage disposal as a class there would probably still be changes in the position of individual persons or firms because the incidence of charges would almost certainly differ to some extent from the incidence of the general rate. At this level however a number of other factors have to be taken into account. The very large discrepancies in the cost of these services which at present exist between areas would be ironed out to a considerable extent by the equalisation of costs over larger areas as a result of the reorganisation the Committee is envisaging. Expenditure is rising. And although the objective in devising a system of charges would be to set them at an economic level, particularly as between industrial users and domestic users, the extent to which the present trade effluent charges meet or fail to meet the true costs of dealing with trade effluents is not known. Whatever assumptions are made about future exchequer assistance to local authorities it would be impracticable to calculate the net effect of all these changes on individual persons or firms.

# POSSIBLE BOUNDARIES FOR REGIONAL WATER AUTHORITIES

## (a) 7 REGIONAL WATER AUTHORITIES

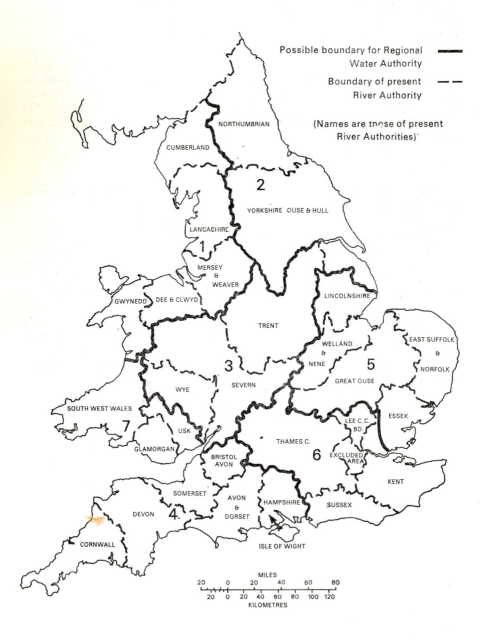

Possible boundary for Regional Water Authority

Boundary of present River Authority

(Names are those of present River Authorities)

# POSSIBLE BOUNDARIES FOR REGIONAL WATER AUTHORITIES

## (b) 13 REGIONAL WATER AUTHORITIES

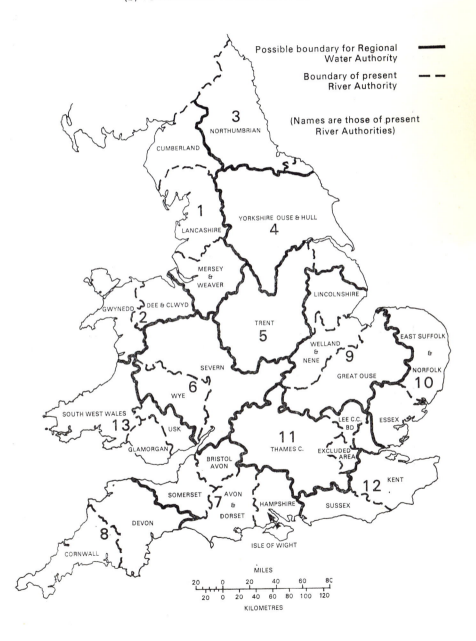

Possible boundary for Regional Water Authority

Boundary of present River Authority

(Names are those of present River Authorities)

3 NORTHUMBRIAN

CUMBERLAND

1 LANCASHIRE

YORKSHIRE OUSE & HULL 4

MERSEY & WEAVER

GWYNEDD

DEE & CLWYD

2

LINCOLNSHIRE

TRENT 5

WELLAND & NENE

EAST SUFFOLK & NORFOLK 10

SEVERN

GREAT OUSE

9

WYE 6

SOUTH WEST WALES

13

USK

GLAMORGAN

BRISTOL AVON

LEE C.C. BD

ESSEX

THAMES C. 11

EXCLUDED AREA

KENT

12

SOMERSET

7

AVON & DORSET

HAMPSHIRE

SUSSEX

DEVON

8

CORNWALL

ISLE OF WIGHT

MILES

20  0  20  40  60  80

20  0  20  40  60  80  100  120

KILOMETRES

105

## DIAGRAMS ILLUSTRATING THE ALTERNATIVE SYSTEMS OF ORGANISATION DESCRIBED IN CHAPTER 5

Separate statutory bodies are shown as boxes formed by continuous lines.

The links between different statutory bodies are shown by continuous lines.

Divisions or functions within a single statutory body are shown by broken lines, as are functional and executive links.

# MULTI-PURPOSE AUTHORITY

Regional Water Authority

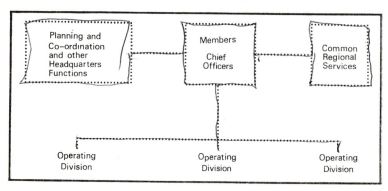

# SYSTEMS OF ORGANISATION BASED ON SINGLE-PURPOSE AUTHORITIES

## SYSTEM A

Regional Water Authority

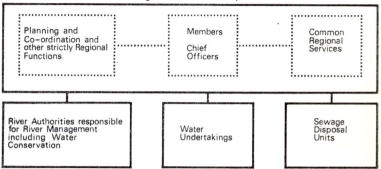

| | | |
|---|---|---|
| Planning and Co-ordination and other strictly Regional Functions | Members Chief Officers | Common Regional Services |

| | | |
|---|---|---|
| River Authorities responsible for River Management including Water Conservation | Water Undertakings | Sewage Disposal Units |

## SYSTEM B

Regional Water Authority

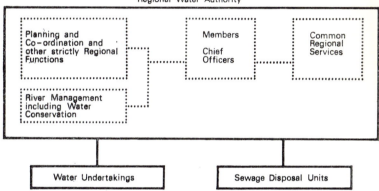

| | | |
|---|---|---|
| Planning and Co-ordination and other strictly Regional Functions | Members Chief Officers | Common Regional Services |
| River Management including Water Conservation | | |

| | |
|---|---|
| Water Undertakings | Sewage Disposal Units |

## SYSTEM C

Regional Water Authority

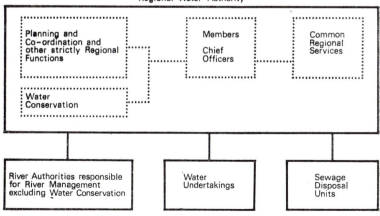

| | | |
|---|---|---|
| Planning and Co-ordination and other strictly Regional Functions | Members Chief Officers | Common Regional Services |
| Water Conservation | | |

| | | |
|---|---|---|
| River Authorities responsible for River Management excluding Water Conservation | Water Undertakings | Sewage Disposal Units |

Printed in England for Her Majesty's Stationery Office by H. O. Lloyd & Co. Ltd., 7/9 Elliott Place, Islington Green, London, N.1. Dd 501896 K68 3/71.